Connected by Water

Robert D Sluka

Contents

Introduction

¹ I will give thanks to you, LORD, with all my heart;

I will tell of all your wonderful deeds.

² I will be glad and rejoice in you;

I will sing the praises of your name, O Most High.

These verses from Psalm 9 express my hope for this book. I look back on all the experiences I have had in the ocean and am filled with gratitude. Early memories of family vacations to Daytona Beach and the Florida Keys sparked a desire to learn more and experience the vast and wonderful deeds of God in the ocean. I didn't have the language to describe these events spiritually or even an understanding of how the ocean could relate to my faith. That came much later as I and then we (Cindy and I and then eventually the kids) embarked on an adventure that would take us to various parts of the Caribbean, the Great Barrier Reef, a remote island in the Maldives, India, Southeast Asia, Kenya, and the beaches of the UK and southern Europe. I met lots of interesting creatures, including many of our species (*Homo sapiens*) who helped me along the path of understanding my faith a little more clearly and how it integrates into a larger whole.

While this is the story of my experiences and only a subset of them, I think the actual subject of the book is the ocean. I hope that you get to know her more through my interactions with the communities, species, and habitats in various locations. I also hope to trace some of the changes in my thinking through time and take you on a journey to understanding a way of thinking about the ocean and its relationship with God including our part in that. I hope that you will increase your love for the ocean, God, each other, and yourself in a way that will cause you to actively participate in ocean conservation.

5

This book represents my memory of events often from long ago. I have tried to get the details correct, but I am sure that I have glossed over or forgotten much. The emphasis is on the experiences, the places, sometimes the people, and the learning rather than an exact, full, and detailed account. My hope is that you will enjoy a trip to far-off places and a desire will grow to get to know better the one who made the oceans and all that is in them. This is my attempt to express in words my thanks to God, to tell of His wonderful deeds in the ocean, and to sing (write) the praise of his name. It certainly has made me glad, and I have rejoiced in all that I have had the privilege of seeing and doing on this amazing blue planet.

Bob Sluka

August 2024

https://sluka.substack.com/

Exuma Cays Land and Sea Park, Bahamas

I found myself staring into the face of a Barracuda as large as myself. I knew I had the best job in the world at that point, but I didn't realize how good it was. Nor did I have words to express what this encounter with a fellow creature meant to me as a whole person. That would come many years later and after much study, reflection, and a whole cast of interesting characters who gave of their time, knowledge, and experience so that I could be whole.

People sometimes ask what I did for my Ph.D. and I usually reply that I counted fish. No really, they ask, what did you do? I counted fish. Of course, I did it in a precise and hopefully accurate way, with a statistical design to the counting which allowed the testing of certain hypotheses and subsequent publication in peer-reviewed journals. But essentially, I was counting fish. I found myself with a Ph.D. in hand from the University of Miami and a postdoc at this same institution working with my Ph.D. advisor. Relatively newly married, Cindy played in local symphony orchestras while I continued to count fish. That is how I found myself about 100 feet deep hanging over much deeper water counting fish in the Exuma Cays Land and Sea Park, Bahamas.

This Park is one of the oldest Marine Protected Areas in the Caribbean, and at the time I did not know that in the distant future, I would be working in one of Africa's oldest protected areas, but that is another chapter. Marine protected areas are places in the ocean that are protected from negative impacts by humans. This can be total protection such that very few, usually scientists, can even enter them, but usually these have some level of use. The Exuma Cays Land and Sea Park is closed to fishing and unlike many other marine protected areas, this is regularly and effectively enforced. At the time of the study in the mid-1990s, we were still trying to understand the value of protection from fishing on coral reef ecosystems. Now this effect is quite well known and is relatively unsurprising – stop all fishing and the fish populations become more abundant, larger, and more diverse. What was hypothesized, but mainly unproven, was that this would also benefit fishers outside of the reserve by two effects called spillover and larval transport. With fish getting more abundant and larger, they produce more eggs – a fish twice the size of another can produce not twice as many eggs, but perhaps hundreds of times as many due to the exponential relationship between size and weight in fish. These eggs are buoyant and float out of the protected area and fish settle and grow in fishable areas to be caught one day. Additionally, many fish have home ranges, areas they live in and generally stay within. With more fish in a marine protected area, they tend to move out more regularly and since there is no sign for them underwater marking the boundaries of the protected area, the fish swim out and are available to fishers along the edges of the park.

The day of the barracuda encounter was a perfect marine biology day. The water was a shade of turquoise that is only found in tropical coral reef ecosystems, the sun was shining, and we were traveling in a small boat from our liveaboard dive boat to the study site. My fellow lab mate Mark Chiappone and I were buddied together – the idea being you always dive with another person for safety – yet we were so comfortable both with each other and being underwater that we parted ways and left for our respective tasks - he to document all the creatures and plants growing on the reef, and me, well, to count fish of course. We could almost have done our work from the boat the water was so clear. Swimming amongst the beauty of that place, we headed towards the point where the flat reef took a distinct 90-degree downward turn and became a wall. The first dive of the day is usually the deepest and that was the case that day. I was looking for grouper, a type of tropical and subtropical fish targeted by fishers for its size, taste, and value. I headed over the wall and began to do my survey hanging suspended over deep water that makes up the Tongue of the Ocean, a deep trench at the edge of the Exuma Park. That is when I noticed something noticing me.

Clipboard laden with underwater paper and pencil in hand, I saw it far below. First, it was just a shadow, perhaps even imagination with the deep blue weighing on my mind. But then it began to grow, and I realized that something was traveling towards me. It grew bigger and then before I could recognize it, shot past my head towards the surface. I looked up and it was staring back at me, right above my head – the barracuda. If you haven't seen one of these underwater you may have either an exaggerated view of the danger I was in or be wondering why I was even concerned. Circumstances often make the experience. This fish was about as big as I am – and I am 6 foot 5 inches tall. Barracudas have very large eyes and a pointed mouth that is full of big teeth. Fish "breathe" in water through their mouths, passing it out across gills held behind gill slits in their head extracting precious oxygen. This, when combined with the aforementioned big teeth results in the natural state of this fish appearing menacing.

We looked at each other for quite some time. The barracuda examining me and I examining her, or could be him, of course. At that time, I remember being grateful. Grateful for the experience and seeing the beauty and worth in this animal neighbor. Grateful that I was living a life that would, hopefully, and eventually, result in the protection of this creature and others like her. However, some of the language I just used to write those sentences was not a part of the original experience but was imported and superimposed onto the experience afterward. I do remember being grateful, but I also know that I would not have thought of that fish as her or neighbor. Possibly not even as a creature, certainly not a fellow creature. This theological language to describe that experience came much later in life, in fact, 10 or 15 years later and in another world.

Detroit, USA

I am not sure if anyone has ever done this, but I imagine if you were to poll marine biologists and ask where they grew up, you would get a distinctly bimodal distribution. There would likely be many marine biologists who grew up in and around the sea. They had always loved the ocean and that was their natural habitat. The other big grouping would be people who grew up far from the sea and who likely discovered a love for the ocean through family holidays, books, or TV. Those in my generation, born in the late 60s or early 70s are highly likely to note the influence of a particular French man – Jacques Yves Cousteau.

It is hard to set the stage for those times when there was no way to record a TV program for later watching and when much of the USA watched the same programs at the same time. *The Undersea World of Jacques Cousteau* was on Sunday nights, and the family gathered to see what adventure he and his intrepid crew were on that week. It brought the ocean into a living room in the suburbs of Detroit and inspired a young boy to dream of the ocean. Later he would have another impact on my life in that he was the co-inventor of the main breathing tool called a regulator used in a Self-Contained Underwater Breathing Apparatus, or SCUBA kit. Diving was just beginning to become a recreational sport, and at the time you had to be 14 to start training. I began the training at 13, turning 14 during the course, and thanks to Mr. Cousteau was off on a lifetime adventure of discovering the underwater world I had seen on the television.

My great-grandmother on my mother's side had come to America with her husband before World War 1. It is often still unclear exactly what my ethnic background is, but much of it is Slavic, particularly from what is now the Czech Republic and Slovakia. The factories in Detroit were attracting a lot of immigration and many of my ancestors came for that reason. There was a growing Slavic community in Detroit and my mother tells of hearing her grandfather praying in Czech each evening through the air ducts in their house. Well, it almost didn't happen. Great-grandmother didn't seem to like America at all! She headed back to the old country after a few kids had been born, leaving them in the care of the wider community and family. However, it seems the looming war changed her mind, and she was on one of the last boats to leave Europe before it became impossible, or likely deadly, to travel the Atlantic.

We were what one might call a religious family, though of the type that would have shunned that term, and if labeled that would have gone into a long explanation about how it is not about religion but a relationship. All true, but just a different type of religion – which is not a bad thing. Religion has been a part of society since humans appeared on the earth. We attended an Assemblies of God church which is part of the Pentecostal movement generally. My experience with organized religion and different types of churches after my childhood leads me to believe that each group has something very good to offer. This is often the focus or organizing principle around which other priorities are focused. Sometimes it is just one's perception, but I found, for example, that in the Anglican Church unity was emphasized over other principles. In direct contrast to that, many of the churches I attended would suggest that truth is the guiding light. Is it unity or truth? Both, of course. But one way of emphasis results in the Anglican Communion, that beautiful, messy group of churches that are working hard to be unified in the face of lots of differences in their version of *truth*. Whereas many Presbyterian denominations have resulted from (significant) differences in what they consider to be truth, deciding that unity cannot be preserved.

Part of the work in preparation for joining some of the Christian work we were a part of was to do batteries of psychological tests. One which I found helpful is the Myers-Briggs test. One of the axes of personality is between Judging and Perceiving. Psychologists, please stop reading here at my butchering of this explanation, but for me, on one end are those who see things in black and white and on the other in a palate of grey. Another aspect of this is that the Judging end of the spectrum wants clear decisions and things nicely demarcated, whereas those of us on the Perceiving end are OK with open-ended options and things remaining unsettled. We like to keep our options open! I end up on the extreme end of Perceiving and seeing the world more like quantum mechanics than Newtonian physics. I think, though of course I would, that the Bible most often presents us with this type of grey, rather than the black and white that many think. It should come as no surprise that studies on pastors and missionaries reveal an overabundance of high-judging personalities! Take unity and truth. They are both strong, consistent, well-developed Biblical constructs and principles. Which one takes precedence? Well, I think if we are going to take the whole Bible and Christian faith seriously, we can't prefer one over the other; we need to hold these both in tension. Holding together this tension between what is perceived as opposites has been a common theme in my life as I have grown and explored the Christian faith living and working for significant periods among other cultures and varieties of faith than my own.

Growing up in a family and church background that took the Bible literally might seem a sheltered and perhaps harsh way to grow up. However, I really do think I won the parent lottery. People often look back and find ways to blame their parents for various things – often rightly so. My experience of reflecting on things is not that way. Were they perfect? Maybe. I grew up with both sets of grandparents knowing each other before my parents even being born. We attended church together and often went out to eat afterward. Christmas was a bit hectic, but amazing as I grew into being a hungry teenager. We would spend Christmas morning at our house, opening presents and eating an amazing breakfast - my mom cooked breakfast for us most mornings with omelets made to order! Then we would go to my mom's side of the family and have an amazing full Christmas lunch with all the trimmings. Then in the late afternoon, on to my dad's side of the family for another huge meal. My dad's parents were known to pray so long before meals that the food often had to be reheated – you never knew when the Spirit would descend.

My dad was an engineer and a thoughtful person who read Frances Schaefer. I think that had a lot of influence on our decisions, especially to move away from the Assemblies church towards a large Presbyterian church nearby. Ward Church was a large church (4-5000 person congregation) in our area and had a big youth work. Interestingly, when I eventually brought Cindy up to visit our family and we married, many people in the church knew her grandfather. He had started his ministry in the Detroit area and was friends with Ward's pastor. The Youth Director Steve Andrews was an important influence in my life supporting both my basketball and growth as a follower of Christ. This was thankfully before most of the worst of the influence of politics and Christian culture on these types of youth groups. In retrospect, you can see the beginnings, and reading the history of these issues you can see the stain. But I think a commitment to reading and understanding the Bible alongside being more of a white-collar, thinking type of congregation created an openness to critique and on many issues of contention the tension was presented, not demonized. A somewhat benign example was that the church did both water baptisms and infant baptisms – along with infant dedications.

Much more could be said of the influence of Steve, the church, my parents, and youth group friends on my spiritual formation. However, I think that for this story, the main way to think about it was that I came out of high school a committed follower of Christ, enthralled with the idea of sharing the exciting relationship I had with Christ, and convinced I understood what that meant. Probably typical of a zealous teenager the world over. That was combined with a decent standing in the high school pecking order through basketball and academics, lending a certain social power and particular confidence. I think that the home life I had, particularly the support of my parents and the wider community provided a base to be able to go out and do new things, to travel, and to thrive in new contexts. There really wasn't anything that I couldn't do if I wanted to do it. Overall, I think that is such a gift. Even now almost 40 years later, I know that if I mess up enough or get in a big enough jam, I can always go home.

I was tall for my age – six feet by grade 5. In America, this means you play basketball, and I thrived in that competitive world. From the age of 10, I probably shot baskets or played in pickup games each day until the age of 18, usually for hours on end including shoveling the snow outside so that I could bounce the ball and shoot in the cold. I excelled and in fact, at the time was the only 9th grader to ever play in a Varsity playoff game in our town. As I excelled and went to basketball camps where university scouts watched us play, everyone thought I would go on to great things. My neighbor across the street was better than I was and a year older. He went off to university on a scholarship and eventually played professionally chiefly in France. He would come back from university, and I remember him only talking about basketball – no surprise there. I am not sure what clicked in my head, but it was part of helping me decide that I didn't want to pursue basketball. Columbia University had flown me out on a recruiting trip, and I received letters daily from universities across the country. One in particular intrigued me – the University of Miami. Spring break in Detroit means a trip to Florida with friends once you can drive. During that time my grandfather was also in Florida and took me to visit UM. I was hooked. They didn't end up offering me a basketball scholarship, but enough of an academic scholarship to make it possible for my parents to pay for the rest – something I am forever grateful to them for providing. Growing up in Detroit you don't think you can study marine biology, but it turns out that UM had one of the best programs in the country, and the newly appointed director, Dr. Kathleen Sealey (then Sullivan), met with me during my visit. That was a relationship that would prove to be pivotal and would impact the direction of much of the rest of my life.

Coral Gables, Florida, USA

The University of Miami is a private university that at the time I first arrived had a reputation for being a party school with a good American football team. It also had one of the best undergraduate marine science programs in the country. You received a double major: marine science and then either biology, geology, chemistry, or physics. It was fairly rigorous, doing the same course work as all the medical school students in biology and being strongly calculus-based. I didn't find the schoolwork hard, though. My advisor was Dr. Sealey, whom I had met during the visit to UM the previous spring. Introductory classes snorkeling in the Florida Keys convinced me that this was indeed the path I wanted to go on.

I joined the SCUBA club and though I didn't dive a lot, mostly due to financial reasons, one club meeting was hugely significant. Dr Sealey was speaking at the meeting and was involved, if I remember right, as one of the advisors. She told us about a trip she was taking to Australia the next summer and wanted to know if anyone was interested. This began a life of raising my hand and volunteering for interesting things. I couldn't understand why so few others wanted to go. I ended up spending six weeks in Australia with Dr. Sealey much of it on Lizard Island, a famous (in the marine biology world) laboratory on a remote island on the Great Barrier Reef. We also visited James Cook University, now considered one of the top marine biology universities in the world, and I would again raise my hand and volunteer to be in the first group of exchange students. Importantly, my time in Australia solidified my connection to Dr. Sealey and I began to help with her research and some of the introductory courses as a mentor. Eventually, I became her first Ph.D. student.

This was the time of *Miami Vice*, *Scarface*, and most of the cocaine coming into America flowing in through the city. South

Beach was dangerous at night; there was not much to do downtown, and tourists would be murdered if they exited the rental car locations the wrong way. When we eventually decided to leave Miami some 10 years later for the Maldives, it was a bit sad that people were worried about our safety simply because it was a Muslim country. We have never been safer than when living in Islamic contexts or in India – the most dangerous thing we did to our kids was put them in the American school system.

Living on the campus of the University of Miami, I was secluded from much of the violence around me. This garden campus is its own entity and there was little reason to leave except to go to the beach on weekends or down to the Keys to dive. I was involved in the Baptist Student Union and InterVarsity on campus. I mostly went to the Baptist church because I could ride my bike there and the guys at the BSU were a lot of fun. We won the intramural volleyball championship one year and I played a lot of beach volleyball as well as pick-up basketball. Interestingly, I almost got involved in a cult. The Boston Church of Christ was very active on campus, especially on our dorm floor. Thankfully someone on the floor pulled me aside and talked with me about it as I was starting to get involved in the initial weeks of school. I think that my time with the various groups on campus including these groups' commitment to engaging with the Hispanic and African American campus fellowship groups helped to broaden my Christian experience. After this time, I have been a bit of a magpie or chameleon in my faith, being able to adsorb and incorporate different traditions and explore the value of each while staying within the main Christian tradition. It is a great privilege to experience different cultures and faith traditions with an open, but thoughtful, mind.

The ocean occupies 71% of our blue planet. When someone learns that you are a marine biologist, they often ask some obscure question about a creature that only lives somewhere you have never been or never studied. In fact, while there is a certain amount of critical information that needs to be conveyed, especially as you go on in science, the main thing you are learning is how to learn. The whole process of science is very different than most people imagine. Anyone who thinks there could be some giant cabal of scientists out there collaborating to put together some fanciful story that will garner them loads of grant money does not understand the system. It usually starts with an observation. For my Ph.D., people had observed that a certain type of fish (grouper) was more abundant in some areas than others. I really was trying to find answers to that simple question through science. Once we had that observation, then we needed information to be able to test that. We can be wrong about what we observe and often see what we are predisposed to see. So, for example, I needed to go to different areas and actually use procedures that are known to produce relatively accurate counts of grouper and test whether or not it is true that grouper are more often found in certain types of places than others. Then the question is why might that be so. Grouper are more abundant in some types of habitats than others. If you design your data collection with some possibilities in mind ahead of time, you can test those ideas as well. Two important factors that impact fish abundance and distribution are the specific qualities of a habitat and the impact of fishing. For a grouper, you will always find more of them on a coral reef than a sand flat. However, you will find more sand gobies on a sand flat than on a coral reef. If we compare coral reefs, then the question becomes are certain types of coral reefs "better" habitat for grouper than others. So, if you design your data collection right and also then collect other information about those coral reefs, you can begin to answer that question. We collected information on several types of coral reefs and collected what is called the rugosity of those sites – how many holes, crevices, and space was there for a grouper to hide in. It turned out that some types of reefs had more grouper than others and those that had more tended to have higher rugosity. That leads to more questions – why would that be? You can imagine many reasons - maybe there is more space for them to rest and hide from their predators or perhaps it provides more space for their prey, or both. You would need a whole other set of studies to find that out. And so, science progresses. Make an observation, collect data to test that observation, develop explanations to describe your results, and then repeat. This is a bit simplified, but I think it illustrates the process of creating new knowledge, rather than the noble, but very different, task of being a science teacher, for example. Science teachers do not create knowledge.

Much of my work has focused on tropical and subtropical habitats, especially coral reefs. However, seagrass beds and mangrove forests have also been habitats I have worked in. Increasingly I have begun to study sandy beaches and intertidal rock pools as well – often for logistical reasons as it is a lot less expensive in time and money to work on the coast. The time in Miami, though, was spent diving the coral reefs of the Florida Keys with shorter forays to the Bahamas and Dominican Republic. Coral Reefs are considered the rainforests of the ocean, though I think that comparison is mostly in light of the relative success of "save the rainforest" campaigns and attempts to mimic their conservation success. There are certain similarities, of course: high diversity, abundance, and amazing beauty. The secret lies in that coral reefs are actually a system of animals and plants living together constantly growing, changing, and being broken down. Corals are animals, related to jellyfish. They produce a calcium carbonate skeleton and mostly reproduce by splitting in two. This provides a structure for other animals to hide in or to try and grow on top of resulting in a maze of creatures with plenty of places for all types of creatures to live out their lives.

After my undergrad degree, I made a short foray back north. My two years at Michigan State were a great transitional time moving from a successful, but fairly unserious student, to someone enchanted by academia. I thought I wanted to go into mathematical modeling of ecosystems, particularly working with fisheries. Much of my master's work was statistically based. Upon cleaning out some of the notes from my classes during that time I marveled at what I used to know. Most of my notes were letters and equations which I couldn't make much sense of anymore. I never published anything from that time, but learned a lot about fisheries and that I would rather be in the tropics!

Just before leaving for Michigan Dr. Kathleen Sealey made a somewhat offhand comment about coming back for a Ph.D. I reached out to her, and she offered me a position. To be honest, it wasn't my first choice. I was hoping to go to the University of Hawaii to study Pacific reefs, but the funding didn't come through in time. I am certainly glad I went back to Miami, turns out my first night back I met my wife-to-be. I don't believe there is one person for you and had I or she made other choices we are just as likely to be flourishing along another path. However, there are certainly a limited number of people who would willingly put up with me. Most of our friends didn't get our relationship as we were at the surface so different, but it has lasted and usually thrived.

I took Cindy to her first football game of her time at university, the big Miami - Florida State rivalry game. She got to experience all that she imagined of a football game in Miami – sweat, beer spilled on her, and very loud and rude chanting. Kathleen was always kind to Cindy and included her whenever she could in our activities. Part of the funding for our work was to have time at a NOAA/NURC laboratory in the Florida Keys. We had, for students, a large food budget to spend on wings and conch fritters each night and stayed in a two-story house on a canal with rooms on one floor and a government-run laboratory/dive shop on the bottom floor. We woke up each day deciding where to go and our tanks were loaded, and the boat driver took us out for a day on the reefs. Cindy didn't usually go out on the boat but used the great acoustics of the upstairs to practice her oboe. There was one memorable "girlfriend's day" where several significant others joined us out on the boat and most spent it trying to overcome seasickness. I took Cindy snorkeling and not for the last time did we swim after sharks rather than fleeing from them.

Part of our work was also running trips for students. There are many advantages and disadvantages to attending a well-known university. Increasingly many argue that the cost is not worth it. Yet not many other universities ran 10-day research cruises diving in the Florida Keys for their students. I helped to teach these classes as an assistant to Dr. Sealey. She made it possible for one of my best friends Shadd Whitehead to come along as a diving safety officer – alas, we had to abort the cruise after a few days due to a hurricane. After we were married, Cindy came along and as a non-diver was assigned less enviable tasks like taking water measurements and counting tourist snorkelers. These cruises were on the Shedd Aquarium's research vessel, and when I had completed my Ph.D. Kathleen threw a party on board for friends and family.

The research was interesting and we worked together as a team to collect data that would go together in publications and help us understand broader issues. Our work on Elbow Reef illustrates this nicely.

Elbow Reef, Florida Keys National Marine Sanctuary USA

Elbow Reef is in the northern Florida Keys off the island of Key Largo. It is now part of the National Marine Sanctuary, but at the time of my work there this had just been declared and a management plan was yet to be implemented. Much of the Florida Reef Tract which stretches from just south of Miami past Key West and towards the Dry Tortugas was formed by two fast-growing species both in the genus Acropora. These are the only two acroporid species in the Caribbean and they tend to grow fast and often form the matrix around which other species grow and thrive. Staghorn coral (*Acropora cervicornis*) is a bit like a weed in that it forms thickets of long, thin branches which provide lots of space for little fish and other creatures to hide. Elkhorn coral (*A. palmata*) grows thicker branches which intertwine and raise the reef off the bottom several meters with crustose coralline algae, sponges, and other creatures breaking down and cementing together the older portions to form a large structure. Wave action and currents shape how these animals grow and in the Florida Keys often form what are called spur and groove reefs. If you look at these reefs from above, you see long, finger-like projections of coral called spurs with sandy patches in between called grooves. This means that you can swim along the sandy bottom grooves with, in the past, towering coral reef on either side.

Designing a study there are several issues which have to be taken into account. The first is thinking through your hypotheses and developing a good question. Once this part is settled, then comes designing a way of collecting information to statistically test those hypotheses. This breaks down into sampling design – where and when do you collect data – and methodology – how do you collect data. The latter involves making sure that you are indeed actually gathering the data that you think you are and that it has both accuracy and precision. If you are estimating the number of grouper on a spur and groove coral reef, you want the number you actually count to reflect the real number of grouper living there – it has to be accurate. You also want it to be precise, meaning in this case that if you were to repeat the survey and the same number of grouper were present you would count a similar number of individuals. The method used in much of field ecology is to count organisms, in this case, grouper, in a set area or for a set amount of time. For small creatures or plants, a quadrat is used which is a square of a certain size scaled to the organism. So, if you are looking for and counting something extremely small, you might only need to use a 10 centimeter by 10 centimeter grid whereas for much coral reef work counting coral colonies, researchers use 1 meter by 1 meter squares. In underwater work, these are often made of PVC pipes that can be assembled underwater allowing ease of travel to the study area and the water to flow into the pipes so that they don't float. For fish and many other larger more mobile organisms, a transect is used which is a rectangular area with the length and width determined by the species. For small coral reef fish that are very abundant, you might use an area of 10 meters by 1 meter whereas for larger species it might need to be 50 meters by 5 meters or even larger. There are lots of varieties and a whole series of papers on biases associated with these methods. The key is to try and do your best to minimize bias by choosing a transect or quadrat of the appropriate size to accurately and precisely measure what you are trying to study.

This blends in nicely with the sampling design as the number and placement of, in this case, transects, will determine if you can answer the questions you are posing. I was interested in the density (number per meter squared) of grouper on different types of coral reefs. First, we needed a few types of coral reefs and we chose the three main reef types in the Florida Keys: patch reefs, spur and groove reefs, and low-relief spur and groove reefs. We would then need to determine the density of grouper on each of these types of reefs and use statistics to determine if the difference among them was more likely due to actual differences or was within what you might expect to happen randomly. However, you can't just go out and do one transect on one reef and that is that. To assume that one 50 meters by 5 meters area count of grouper is representative of that particular reef or even that one reef is representative of all reefs is not usually a good assumption. This means that you have to replicate transects among all the types of reefs and even within one reef itself. Ideally, you do this in a random way so that your own bias in choosing where to survey doesn't impact the count. So, for example, you might choose three spur and groove reefs and three patch reefs to survey and conduct five transects on each of these reefs. This would allow you to compare the density of grouper on spur and groove reefs versus patch reefs and among reefs of each of these types.

Additionally, we didn't know if the counts might change over time, so we needed to repeat our samples at other times of the year to account for potential seasonality. This led to a complicated statistical design which today can easily be computed probably on a phone. At the time, though, we needed to use a mainframe computer at the university and the most advanced statistical programs. Now the thing that can be most challenging in all of this is that all this data collection must be completed underwater!

At this point, I had been diving for several years recreationally. However, scientific diving is a different type of diving – one where you would often be in remote places, working independently of the recreational diving safety net, and often doing complicated activities or carrying lots of things. Universities have developed programs for training divers and the University of Miami had a great Dive Safety program and officer in Rick Gomez. We took the equivalent of a Rescue Diver course with more scientific-specific topics included along the way and eventually were certified as a scientific diver. For one part of our project, we wanted to explore deeper areas of the

Florida Keys and selected Elbow Reef as one of the sites. Most of our work was conducted shallower than 20 meters (60 feet). Pressure, volume, and temperature are all interrelated so a cylinder of 80 cubic liters of air will last longer at shallower depths. Essentially, the pressure on your body increases by the weight of the entire atmosphere every 10 meters (30 feet). Standing on the surface of the planet you have 1 atmosphere of pressure on your body. At 10 meters depth, you have 2 atmospheres. What this means practically is that your lung volume remains the same at the planet's surface or at 10 meters and so you take in an equal volume of air, but that air at 10 meters is at higher pressure and so it has twice as many air molecules in each breath. A SCUBA tank will last half as long at 10 meters than if you were breathing it at the surface. At 30 meters then, it is four times the pressure of the earth's surface, and that same tank, all things being equal, would last a quarter of the time. What this means from a practical point of view in terms of collecting data is that the deeper you go, the less time you have to do your work.

Then there is the issue of nitrogen. Many people think that SCUBA tanks have oxygen in them, but they are simply purified air. That means that most of what you are breathing is nitrogen – about 79%. You naturally have a certain amount of nitrogen dissolved in your body at the earth's surface. With pressure, more of it dissolves into your bloodstream. Now recall what I just said about pressure and volume. Those tiny bubbles of nitrogen go into your bloodstream at depth and then as you rise to the surface, they increase in size with the decreasing pressure. If you go slow enough and don't have so much in your bloodstream, the bubbles will come out of your blood and not be a problem. However, if you go up too fast or if too much is in your blood and you don't take that into account by making additional stops along the way, then the bubbles can come out of solution in a way that can cause The Bends. This is a condition where these bubbles gather often in joints and cause a lot of pain and possibly permanent damage if not treated. One way of dealing with this is to adjust the amount of nitrogen in the tank called nitrox diving. The amount of nitrogen is reduced by increasing the amount of oxygen from about 21% to somewhere around 32-36%. That small change means that diving in depths up to about 40 meters (120 feet) can not only be safer but last longer by reducing potential nitrogen impacts on the body. It is much more common today in recreational diving, but at the time in the early 90s, there were no recreational certifications for this.

You can see that there is a lot of planning involved in scientific diving! We had a plan then to extend our normal sets of reef types to a deeper area at Elbow Reef which would allow us to determine if there were any significant differences in deeper areas. Our study species, grouper, were known to move offshore with age and we wanted to know if larger individuals or different species lived in these slightly deeper depths of 25-40 meters. We had our tools for observing them and the scientific diving training and nitrox gear to be able to do it safely and as efficiently as possible. So what did we find? Here is the abstract of the paper we published on it in 1998 in the Bulletin of Marine Science.

We examined the density. size and species distribution of groupers in three habitats on an inshore-to-offshore transect across Elbow Reef, Florida Keys: high-relief spur-and-groove (4-9 meters depth), relict spur-and-groove (10-20 meters), and deep fore reef slope (21-30 meters). Physical relief was greatest in the high-relief spur-and-groove (up to 3 meters), lowest in the relict spur-and-groove habitat (0.5-1 meters), and intermediate in the deep fore-reef slope habitat (1-1.5 meters). Benthic coverage in the three habitats was dominated by algae (>30%). There were significant differences in the density, size, and species distribution of groupers among the three habitats. Graysby, *Epinephelus cruentatus*, was numerically dominant, constituting 82-91% of individuals observed. Black grouper, *Mycteroperca bonaci*, and Nassau grouper, *E. striatus*, were more abundant in high to moderate-relief habitats, whereas red hind, *E. guttatus*, was more abundant in the low-relief habitat. The size distribution was shifted towards smaller sizes in the lowest relief habitat and towards larger sizes in areas with greater (>0.5 meters) vertical relief. We suggest that fishing pressure in the Florida Keys has resulted in an offshore grouper assemblage dominated by graysby, a small grouper species (<40 centimeters total length) that is not targeted by fishermen, and that habit selection and biological interactions have significantly influenced the ecological structure of the grouper assemblage of this coral reef.

What this essentially means is that we were able to compare what and how many grouper were in each of the three types of coral reef habitat and indeed found statistically significant differences. Based on the sizes and species differences we found among reefs and our knowledge of fishers habits, we suggested that the reason we found the results we did was 1) due to fishers targeting larger individuals and 2) fish "choosing" to be in certain habitats that had lots of places to hide.

If you made it through this chapter, I hope you can see that there is a lot that goes into "counting fish" to answer a specific question, but more generally you can see the process of science including the point of publishing new information that no one ever knew before.

Great Barrier Reef, Australia

Mention the word Australia to any marine biologist – or almost any person for that matter – and it conjures up images of exotic wildlife and, of course, the Great Barrier Reef. After raising my hand to volunteer at that SCUBA club meeting, preparations began to spend six weeks there with Dr Sealey. There were six of us assisting her in a research project to study echinoderms (the group that includes starfish and sea urchins) at Lizard Island Research Station. This is a well-known marine research facility located on an island – with lots of BIG lizards as in six-foot monitor lizards. This provided easy access and facilities for data collection on beautiful reefs. It was my first experience at a research station, and I thoroughly enjoyed it. We spent the days diving around the island collecting data and then coming back, filling tanks for the next day, and processing the data and samples.

One of the little-known features of marine biology is the time it takes to deal with the data that has been collected. I usually say that for every day I am out in the field, as it is called, collecting data, there are at least four days processing that data. Sometimes you are collecting a sample or a specimen and the point of going into the field is to take these samples. Or in my case, you came back with data sheets that needed to be gone over for completeness and often overwritten in pen as the pencil used underwater on the underwater paper would fade in time or might be difficult to read in the future. Data then must be entered into a computer for future analysis and then when there is enough to test your hypotheses you have to do the analysis and write up your results. It also costs a decent amount to go to these places to do the work and so, many researchers adopt an all-out effort approach and come back from these trips engaged and excited by their work, but often exhausted.

The island itself was magical with huge monitor lizards

roaming the place and a hill challenging enough to take some effort to climb giving a great view of the reef's amazing variety of blue hues. It also solidified my student-mentor relationship with Dr Sealey. She took a very different attitude towards students than many professors, though is probably more typical of field ecologists/marine biologists than lab scientists. We spent significant time together in remote places learning to rely on each other for comradery and for our safety. Before the time on Lizard Island, we rented an offroad vehicle and drove to the northernmost point on the Cape York Peninsula – if you think of Australia on a map, that is the pointy bit in the northeast reaching out towards Papua New Guinea. We camped in the bush and visited beautiful rainforests and remote beaches. We would have to stand guard for each other watching for saltwater crocodiles as we bathed in rivers. One memorable day after lots of rough and ready food, we came across a hamburger stand in the middle of nowhere advertising a burger "with the lot". Who knew that a hamburger with bacon, cheese, pineapple, beetroot, and egg on it could taste so good!

Three memories of that trip stick out in my mind. The first was a night dive. Diving at night is exciting and often allows you to see creatures that are hiding during the day. Coral polyps come out of their cups extending their tentacles to feed which gives them a fuzzy look compared to the smoothness of their daytime garb. Many fish rest in crevices and holes with parrotfish creating a mucus bubble around themselves so that predators cannot smell them. Yes, fish smell. The cardinalfish and squirrelfish that hide in holes during the day are out in number. Sharks, rays, and eels are also more active at night. The other feature of a night dive is that it is dark. This means that you need an underwater flashlight to illuminate all this diversity. So, when you are diving, you can see clearly that which is in the beam of your light, but the rest of the world around you is dark. This often leads to startling encounters when you get that feeling and turn the light behind you to find something interesting. In this case, I was diving in relatively shallow water and turned the beam of my light from the work area to see a set of eyes coming towards me. Initially, I was fairly concerned as there was quite some distance between those eyes, and wondered about a big shark. It turned out to be a beautiful stingray swimming past, but still startling when unexpected. A similar event occurred a few years later when spending several weeks on a remote Bahamian Island studying grouper movement patterns. I drew the short straw that night and was out in a channel collecting data snorkeling alone. I went to the surface to take a deep breath and then started to dive down only to find a very large lemon shark swimming right underneath me right in the beam of my light.

The second experience I remember related more to the diving experience and having to pressurize your ears at depth. Pressure increases with depth and if you have ever tried to swim to the bottom of a swimming pool you will know that without equalizing your ears it will be very painful. Water pressure increases and pushes on your eardrum and since it is a sensitive membrane connected to lots of nerves to allow you to hear, it hurts! However, your nose and mouth are connected to your inner ear through tubes. You can create a small amount of back pressure equalizing the inner ear pressure to the outside water pressure making it possible to be at depth with no ear pain. Now imagine if those tubes get clogged by say a cold. Now there is no way to equalize your ears which is why divers are advised strongly not to dive with a cold. Sometimes you must or sometimes the tubes get blocked during a dive – which is what happened to me. I descended quite happily equalizing my ears and was able to collect lots of data. But on trying to ascend to the surface it became extremely painful. The problem with just going to the surface and bearing the pain is that your eardrum can rupture and then you are done with diving – certainly for the foreseeable future, but also possibly forever. So thankfully I could make it to fairly shallow water where I didn't have to use much air and slowly, slowly worked at using the water pressure to clear those tubes and get rid of the pressure building inside my inner ear. Finally, there was a loud squeak as the air rushed out into my nose and mouth and I could get out of the water.

The last experience was also potentially my last experience ever! I saw this beautiful small octopus in shallow water. Octopuses are extremely intelligent and sometimes will "play" with you. On other dives in other places, an octopus has explored my hand and arm with its tentacles and I had something of a "My Octopus Teacher" experience. The thing about this octopus was that it had blue rings. This means it is extremely poisonous! These octopuses only live in the Indo-Pacific region, so I had never encountered them before and for some reason hadn't realized or perhaps in the moment forgot about the deadly bite. Thankfully as I reached my hand for it Dr Sealey made sure I stopped. These are gorgeous creatures to look at, but not to touch.

I returned to the University of Miami after those six weeks heading right to my dorm room. I remember meeting my new roommate and to his horror exclaiming that I had just returned from Australia and pouring out sand accumulated in my backpack onto our dorm room floor. Much of my life I have tracked sand into my living spaces and even now in Florida end up brushing it out of our bed most nights. This was not to be my last trip to Australia. Kathleen (Dr Sealey, whom I was now on a first name basis with) had set up an exchange program with James Cook University, the premier marine biology university in Australia, and located close to the Great Barrier Reef. When the time came, I once again raised my hand and became one of three exchange students to pioneer that program. When I looked later at one of the photos taken on my first trip to Australia with Kathleen, it turned out that I had photographed my eventual dorm during a visit to the university.

I packed up my bags, including my bicycle or push bike as it was to be called in the land of Oz, and flew across the world for 10 months of Australian education. In many ways going to Miami had been cross-cultural with so many nationalities and the prevailing Latin American flavor of that great city. This was, however, total immersion into another culture – the first of many. It is a privilege, to anticipate future chapters, to have lived on four continents and traveled significantly to two others. James Cook University is on the coast in north Queensland and at the time was gaining a reputation for marine biology. This was helped significantly by the headquarters of the Great Barrier Reef Marine Authority and the Australian Institute of Marine Science being headquartered in the same town – perhaps underlying its basic character uncreatively called Townsville. I learned about meat pies, sausage rolls, and Vegemite all culinary delights that would later be reintroduced in a slightly different avatar in England. I learned about a more collectivist society as I had excellent, and thankfully not often used, universal health care. I remember resting my arm on the edge of the door with the window rolled down driving across town. Something most Americans would not think twice about. My friend asked me to remove it so that the police wouldn't stop us. I was quite confused and remember some callous diatribe I launched into about personal freedoms. Personal safety is a community issue in a society where everyone literally pays for your stupidity or lack of good choices. Now I think it's a small price to pay for never having to worry about medical debt or paying our outrageously high insurance premiums. But I digress. Suffice it to say, I was likely an ugly American, but my friends put up with me.

The university had a scientific diving program and I signed up immediately. This resulted in great opportunities to help out Ph.D. students and professors on their projects. I also had to turn down a few research cruises that are still painful to remember missing. One of the first trips I went on was as part of the Australian Institute of Marine Science's Crown of Thorns starfish monitoring program. Coral bleaching is getting a lot of attention right now, but that was not always the case not only because the problem wasn't as bad as it is now. Many reefs around the world that are being "decimated" by bleaching are only shadows of their former selves due to other causes. In the late 1980s when I was in Townsville there was a major problem with fishing on the GBR and only recently had it been protected from overfishing through a series of marine protected areas. One of the species of fish that was no longer abundant was an emperor fish which was about the only species that ate Crown of Thorns starfish. The name says it all – it really does look like a crown of thorns and those thorns have venom that causes swelling of hands if touched by mistake – as I learned the hard way. With its main predator in decline, populations of this species would swell into plagues and decimate reefs. Additionally, though the research at the time was just being done, it was learned that nutrient runoff from agriculture on land was causing algae blooms that then resulted in higher survival rates of starfish larvae – which feasted on the plankton.

I remember laying in the back of the live aboard dive boat heading offshore in huge waves. Each day we would do 4 or 5 dives on amazing reefs on the outer GBR. The concepts were similar to what I explained in the Exuma Park chapter – we used transects that gave us accurate and precise estimates of Crown of Thorns starfish density and did this over multiple reefs and reef types to understand the distribution on this part of the Great Barrier Reef. Living and working on board a research vessel was an exciting time of learning, diving till exhaustion, and gaining experience in underwater research.

Ph.D. students often did research at the local offshore coral reefs surrounding Magnetic Island. I remember helping one grad student study the corals using a university boat. We arrived at the site and realized that we had forgotten an important piece of equipment – the mount that holds a SCUBA tank on your back. I ended up diving while holding a tank in one arm and doing the research with the other. On another dive on my previous trip to Lizard Island, I remember a mask strap breaking and not having a spare with us in the small boat and having to dive holding the mask on. Unless safety is severely compromised, and even sometimes when it is, the data takes priority over comfort, convenience, and safety. My friend Tirra was over from America on a Rotary scholarship and mapping intertidal corals on Magnetic Island. We spent many a fun day taking the ferry over to the island to arrive at low tide and map out corals having a nice beach picnic lunch together.

Overall, I think that my year in Australia gave me skills and confidence as a marine biologist in training. I learned much from the culture that set me on a path of exploration and adventure. There was a cost to this – being away from friends and family for a long time – but I learned that often the price is worth paying.

Maldives

Cindy and I had been married for about a year and a half when an email arrived. She had finished her Master's degree in oboe performance and I had finished my Ph.D. I was applying for university jobs and receiving very few responses and when I did it was usually negative. She was playing professionally in several orchestras in South Florida and teaching oboe at Miami Dade Community College. My postdoc brought me to the Bahamas but was mostly Miami-based and gave me time to write up several publications.

Several summers before this, I spent 10 weeks in Maldives researching grouper populations. This was at the invite of Steve Holloway a marine biologist who along with Dr Norman Reichenbach, now of Liberty University, were working to develop sea cucumber and algae mariculture there. Maldivians are great fishers and like to dabble in agriculture on their personal land, but aquaculture was not something developed in the country at that time. The Asian luxury market for sea cucumbers had wiped out most of these animals throughout the country in just a few short years. The hope was to develop mariculture to continue to provide livelihoods. You probably don't realize it, but much of what you eat or drink has an ingredient derived from marine algae – carrageenan. This is a stabilizer and basically keeps solids in suspension – so think of a chocolate milk bottle. If it didn't have a stabilizer, then the chocolate would come out of suspension and settle to the bottom of the bottle. Several species of algae are grown in ocean-based "farms" to provide the raw material for this chemical. Steve and Norm were experimenting with developing these industries in the country and were conducting research trials to determine how to better do this. I had, and have, no interest in mariculture, but it was a fantastic excuse to go to the Maldives and scuba dive collecting some information on grouper in an area where there had been little research.

The Maldives is well known for its beautiful islands and coral reefs. Picture your idealized small island with coconut palm trees, surrounded by white sand beaches and beautiful blue water. Until fairly recently, these dreams sold to tourists were ones that the local population could not participate in. The Maldives is made up of about 1200 islands, arranged in circular atolls. This latter word is in fact, the only Maldivian word in the English language. Charles Darwin wrote a book on the formation of coral reefs in the 1800s which is still essentially correct. He names these circular rings of islands "atolls" in English after the Maldivian word atolu. The Maldives is an Islamic Republic and there was intentional effort by the government, which also functions as the protector of Islam in the country, to separate tourists from islanders. So ultimately about 80 or so islands were given over to tourist resorts and to this day, if you stay in most resorts in the country, you will have the island to yourself and the other guests of that hotel. Until recently, it was not possible to visit villages except the capital city Male' without a permit and Maldivians who didn't work on a resort couldn't visit them either.

I was able to collect enough data on the density and diversity of grouper to publish one paper with Norm Reichenbach and presented that research at the Snapper Grouper Symposium in Mexico. Someone secured me a scuba compressor and tanks and I had brought my own dive gear. So I made probably 50 dives over those weeks. When I look at my dive log it says that my dive buddy was somebody named Jesus. Yep, data took precedence over safety and I dove alone. Most of the work was in very shallow water and away from dangerous currents or the deeper drop-offs the Maldives is known for, but for one memorable dive, I decided to go to 50 meters (150 feet) just to see what is there. Nitrogen narcosis kicked in and I remember shaking my head underwater and realizing I was daydreaming at the bottom of the sea.

I stayed on an "uninhabited" island, which meant that a Maldivian had rented it from the government and was developing a business on it. In this case, it was an aquarium fish export business. The island which could be circumnavigated in about 10 minutes by foot had buildings full of aquarium tanks. The design was such that the ocean flooded the floor of the building during high tides, and I remember one evening sitting under the light of a naked bulb with several workers, mostly from poorer South Asian countries, eating fish and rice. I had brought some Kool-Aid packets with me, as most American expats of that time did, and its vibrant blue color shone out of our glasses. The tide was in, and we sat with our feet submerged in the seawater and the fish tanks bubbling in the background. Not for the first time in my life did I wonder how in the world I ended up in that place.

This was in my mind when I read the email sent to us. Cindy had never traveled to Maldives or really spent much time in a much poorer country. We were invited to go live on a remote Maldivian island with Norm and his wife Susan and two small children for the next year. Steve Holloway and his wife Kitty were moving away, and Norm and Sue wanted to spend at least another year there but preferred to have some company. This would be a great opportunity for me, but not so good for an oboeist. In fact, not good at all. We talked and prayed. I think the main thought in our mind from a practical perspective was that it would be so easy to put our heads down on the table where we were discussing this decision and wake up 5 years later with everything exactly the same. Cindy had always wanted to move overseas, particularly to try and serve a spiritual cause, so it wasn't so surprising for her to say yes. We made the decision together, but career-wise, she bore the cost. Within six months, we would pack up our lives in Miami and embark on an adventure we could never have predicted.

We made our decision to move to Maldives in February of 1996 and would end up moving in August. However, I had a few more things to finish. One was my postdoc, writing up a major report and analysis of the value of the Exuma Cays Land and Sea Park for grouper conservation. Our lab was also contracted to assess and describe the coral reefs offshore of Guantanamo

Bay in Cuba. US military bases were working with The Nature Conservancy to see if there was a way with all their land and sea to contribute towards conservation. I spent several weeks on the base diving all day long and making sure not to come up on the other side of the fence in Cuban territory. My fins decided to die there, and I bought a new Mares set at the base store. These are the fins that I still use to this day, good after close to 30 years of diving. Lastly, I attended the International Coral Reef Symposium in Panama.

Every four years, coral reef scientists from around the world gather to share their work and set some priorities for coral reef work globally. It is now a huge event with thousands of participants. This one was the 8th such event. I had, by chance, attended the 6th one in Australia, though I was one of the students helping scientists run their slides (yes, really slides at that time) earning a little extra money during my time at James Cook University where it was being held that year. In more recent years I have had my name on papers presented by others as our work particularly in Kenya has been presented by Dr Benjamin Cowburn. My talk in Panama was on grouper ecology based on my work in the Bahamas. I was interested in attending a talk by scientists from the Maldives, given that I was leaving for that country soon. They talked generally about the situation there in Maldives and ended their talk by saying what they needed most was someone to come to their country and study grouper! I excitedly went up to them after and explained that I was studying grouper and was indeed coming to their country very soon. I saw this experience as a real confirmation that we were moving in the right direction.

It is always dangerous to look for signs from God and certainly to, as some do, demand them before moving forward. However, in our path forward in life we have often found that there are moments that act as anchors when we despair. All life has these moments of despair, but I think particularly lives where you are not following a traditional path. It was in the future when things were difficult that we were able to look back at that time in Panama and remember that request by the Maldivian scientists.

Both Cindy and I grew up in churches that were very supportive of missionaries – which is how we saw ourselves at the time. It was also at the beginning of the movement within many US churches that began to focus on seeing new churches started, particularly in places where there were none. Maldives certainly qualified as there was and still is no church in the country nor has there ever been. We probably had illusions (delusions) of grandeur at the time that we would fix that. My thinking on the Christian faith and particularly the role of my science was moving forward a little, but still grounded in dualistic and anthropogenic thinking. Science wasn't now just a "hobby" where I could do something fun and get paid for it so that I could do the real Christian work of service during other times, but now it gave entry to a place where we might be the first Christians someone encountered. It was still very much a means to a different end. Our churches and many individuals signed up to help us financially so that we could travel to and live in the Maldives. This set a pattern for the future where for the past almost 30 years we have lived from the generosity of others who believe in what we are doing and particularly in us. This has allowed us to serve, and we have never wanted for our needs for which we are hugely grateful. It also allowed me to do a lot of research with few science dollars as I didn't have to raise my salary from the science work. That meant that I could pursue topics that were of interest or importance, but for which there weren't huge amounts of money. Several thousand dollars of research funds could keep me going for some time.

There were some significant conservation issues in the Maldives, and I won a fairly prestigious fellowship from the Wildlife Conservation Society to fund my research. Hundreds of millions of people in the world directly make their living from the sea. Many of these are what is known as artisanal fishers going out in small boats, often kayaks with no motors or even just swimming offshore, to provide their daily fish. On the other extreme are the huge industrial fishing fleets that scour the ocean and catch fish by the billion. Artisanal fishers can sometimes make significantly more money catching specific ocean creatures that are then sold to a luxury market where wealthier people will spend lots of money for a single individual. The live fish food trade is one of these markets that operates in many places, but especially in a large circle of water centered on Hong Kong and radiating out as far as necessary to provide these special fish. At the time, a kilogram of fresh tuna at the beach in Maldives might fetch 1.5 Maldivian Rupees whereas a live grouper caught, held in a cage, and then sold live to a collecting boat from Hong Kong might fetch 200 times that amount. There is a huge incentive to catch the very last fish and in fact, rarity confers value in many cases so perversely as the fish populations decline, the prices go up causing even more people to try and catch the dwindling population.

At the time, there hadn't been much, if any study of grouper in the Maldives, and boats from Hong Kong were showing up looking for fish. The market for sea cucumbers had recently been in the government's mind in terms of management and essentially all sea cucumbers in the country within diving or snorkeling ranges were wiped out by unregulated fishing. I wanted to know basic information – what species of grouper were there, how many, where did they live and how far did they move. This is a good example of taking one set of skills learned in one place (counting fish in Florida) and applying it to a new place and problem. The fishery, species, and types of coral reefs were all different, but the same methodology could be applied to be able to answer some important questions for managing the growing fishery.

A small laboratory had been built on Gan Island in Laamu Atoll in the south of Maldives, outside the tourist zone. We had to have special permission to do this and our sponsors, The Oceanographic Society of Maldives, helped facilitate the process. Gan is the largest island in the country, but still only about 1.5 by 8 km in size. Our village Thundi was one of three on the island which also included the airport for the atoll. There were few places to get away to do something special for a date and the airport restaurant served as one of these and Cindy and I rode a moped to get some space. Almost no one on the island spoke English, which was great for learning Maldivian, but it did result at times in being in places where English songs were played without the others around us realizing that they had extremely rude lyrics. At the time, there were more language-learning resources for Klingon than for Dhivehi, the Maldivian language. By the end of the first year, I could write notes in Maldivian to my dive buddies underwater in their language. There is a different set of characters and it is written right to left – so though they understood based on their response to my written underwater notes, I imagine that there was also lots of confusion. Thundi had about 800 residents at the time, and we lived in a home called Blue Heaven. The village had electricity from about 6pm till midnight and we would crawl under our mosquito nets in good time for the power going out so we didn't get bit up. One small lizard seemed to find a way, though, to press the mosquito net down enough so that it could lay on my head and warm itself through the night.

Maldivians are very social and privacy is almost an unknown concept. It took time to get used to people walking into your house or even going into your bedroom to wake you up so they could ask you something. In a Muslim society, shoes were not worn inside, and we eventually learned that if we wanted a quiet afternoon nap, we could close and lock our bedroom door (which opened to the outside of the house), pulling in our shoes so that people thought we were out. Many a time I would be just getting into a good book and a friend would walk by, see me there alone and thus presumably not happy, and would come in for a chat or invite me along. This 24/7 lifestyle would be ours both in Maldives and soon in India for almost 10 years. There is something beautiful about the communal life and living always out in the open socially, but it also can be wearing. Much is made about the differences between event-orientated societies and time-orientated societies, but I found the issue of communal/social obligations a much more difficult difference to navigate. Arguably, Maldives was on the extreme end of this as, it should be said, was America. I had learned some of the ideas behind a more communal approach to some aspects of society in Australia, but this was still a steep learning curve.

"I think I have invited our landlord over for dinner," Cindy said on one of our first days in the village. Someone had given us some squid and we were going to try and figure out how to cook it – now, it seems, with an audience. It turned out terrible, but the result was that it connected us with that family much more deeply, and they gave some lessons on how to cook with what was available locally. Cross-cultural communication is always fraught with difficulties. In retrospect, though we were trained significantly in how to try and communicate well across cultures, I now realize that I was mostly translating. Meaning that I thought I understood certain principles, particularly spiritual ones, and needed to contextualize these to the Maldivian culture and language. But what I didn't realize was how many of those principles were already contextualized to my American culture. Perhaps one of the ways to illustrate this is the difference between a guilt-based culture, like many Western ones, and an honor-shame culture, like many Eastern ones.

Take the Biblical story of the woman who was bleeding and Jesus' healing of her. Now, not only is there a gender issue here in that most males wouldn't really understand the implications and personal nature of this story since we do not menstruate. But then layer on top of our guilt-based culture and this is mainly portrayed as a story of Jesus' power and ability to heal. We don't understand the ideas of ritual impurity and that at the time, Jesus by touching the woman was under Jewish law ritually unclean and, like the woman, unfit to worship at the Temple. You can say to yourself – "but so what?" which probably belies your own lack of living in an honor and shame-based culture. This was a hugely significant event in the woman's life in terms of her restoration to ritual purity and Jesus making a much bigger statement about Himself than just that he could heal. Communicating across cultures requires trying to understand the mindset or worldview of the person you are speaking with, and not just translating words but trying to see that story or idea through their eyes. I don't think I was, or am, very good at that.

Some will argue that there is only one Christian worldview – meaning that everyone who reads the Bible and follows Christ should think the same way. This really does not do justice to what a worldview is nor the reality that a worldview is a multi-layered identity made up of many ways of seeing the world. The Bible informs and shapes our worldview, but we don't derive it from our faith.

As a digression of sorts, and while I am still unsure of the multiverse, I think we all live in separate universes. I am looking out at some green trees in our back garden as I write this. While there is a somewhat objective view of what "green" is based on wavelengths of light, if you were to be sitting next to me right now the green you would see would be very different from what I am seeing. The view would not change, but I also would look at the green of my passionfruit vine and see the hope of that wonderful fruit. You may have tasted passionfruit, but you don't have the memory of paying way too much for a few passionfruit in England to give to our kids as Christmas presents and the joy of them opening them up and tasting that amazing nectar. You don't remember the first time of tasting passionfruit juice at a farm in Brazil 30 years ago and the memories of that trip. I could go on but looking at the green of that passionfruit vine I am sensing, smelling, and remembering something very different from anyone else on the planet. We go about thinking everyone is having the same experience as we are and that there is some objective reality that is the same for everyone – I just don't think that matches experience or what we understand now about our senses.

The beauty of underwater Maldives is hard to overhype. One day heading out to a dive spot to work on the grouper project we saw a superpod of dolphins – this appeared to be 10-15 pods of dolphins churning the water moving through one of the channels. We jumped in and it was amazing to see these creatures swimming in their family units. You would be surveying coral cover and your buddy would point behind you and a majestic manta ray would be swimming past. A favorite memory is of a zebra shark (*Stegosoma tigrinum*) lying on the sandy bottom in crystal clear water. Such a beautiful creature. I began to do some surveys of butterflyfish as well, partly because no one had done it there and the other was to be able to identify and spend time watching these small, colorful fish.

My friend Dr. Margaret Miller and I received a small grant from the National Geographic Society which paid for her to come to Maldives for several weeks. She is an expert in coral reef ecology and has done many studies on herbivory – the process of animals eating plants. At that time so little was known from the Maldives that any information was important – in fact, Margaret and I published a paper that had basically negative results. We had surveyed crown of thorns starfish, a coral predator, across the atoll and really only found a couple individuals. But this was at the height of Crown of Thorns outbreaks, particularly in Australia and it was important to know that they were not at that time a threat in this area. The main experiment Margaret and I wanted to complete necessitated a lot of setup work, including getting a lot of metal caging from the capital down to our island by boat. We set up the experiment to look at herbivory on corals but were thwarted by an early-season storm destroying the setup. With science, this can happen often. However, we regrouped and figured out a way to investigate the long-term impacts of nutrient enrichment on lagoon reefs. A friend had noted that when flying over the country fishing villages had lagoons full of seagrass. This was not normally the case and we wondered why. Most Maldivians eat tuna, not reef fish and travel hours offshore to catch particularly the skipjack tuna using fishing poles. It is an amazing site to watch a boatload of Maldivian men with very long wooden poles with a line and a barbless hook on the end scatter baitfish into the deep ocean and cause a feeding frenzy of skipjack tuna. Then they put the hook into the middle of the frenzy and pull out an individual, flipping them into the boat hold and returning the hook for another all in one motion. The boat returns to the village beach and the tuna are gutted on the shore with the next high tide taking these fish parts out into the lagoon. We quantified seagrass cover offshore of these fishing villages and compared them to villages that primarily did non-fishing work and to uninhabited islands, with Margaret taking sand samples back to Miami to test for nutrients. It seems that over hundreds of years, the small input of these nutrients had changed the nature of the lagoons offshore of fishing villages. Not what we set out to test, but an important result nonetheless.

Maldives is an Islamic Republic and at the time, it was illegal to talk about religion even among friends. We knew this and in fact was one of the reasons we wanted to be there Though I would think about it differently now, we were driven by a zeal to share our faith. This meant that we would spend a lot of time hanging out with folks in the tea shops – or rather I would, women weren't really allowed. The men would sit in these string chairs that line up together in a row and chew betel nut, something that I enjoyed. We celebrated the main Islamic festivals with our friends and even fasted during Ramadan – something our friends never really believed. We couldn't be bothered to get up in the middle of the night to eat a late meal under cover of darkness and so I ended up losing about 30 pounds off an already skinny body. Breaking the fast each night with friends was a joyous time.

Islam colonized much of south and southeast Asia and in the Maldives like many other countries, there remains tradition and culture that predates becoming Muslims. One of the Islamic festivals was quite an eye-opener for me. Remembering that what is occurring is all happening in the Maldivian language which we were still at a very early stage of learning, we entered into the village square near the tea shop to find a court scene unfolding. A table of judges, with requisite long white wigs, were sitting and holding some sort of trial. I eventually was called up and like many accused of taking something – in the Maldivian language it was called a kordi. This, it turns out was a wooden structure that was built just for this circumstance. Eventually, someone from another village, who volunteered for this role, was declared guilty and sentenced to dress as a woman the following day and dance his way through the village. At each house, some money was put out front and as he danced, with anatomically correct features though clothed, he received his pay. I was never sure what it all meant and not exactly how I expected to celebrate the end of the fasting month!

We had only gone to Maldives with a one-year commitment to check it out. After much prayer, we decided we wanted to make a long-term commitment, which we perceived at that time as for the rest of our lives. It is very hard to understand at a young age – I had just turned 30 – that there are likely to be many phases to life. In our case, about every 10 years or so I tend to move on to something related, but new. This meant about 10 years in Miami, 10 in South Asia, 11 in the UK, and now going on seven in central Florida. I can see the thread in my life through all of this.

Wildlife Conservation Society, the group that gave me a research grant for the year, enjoyed my work enough to offer me two years of support to do whatever I wanted. I started studying spawning aggregations of grouper and Napoleon wrasse in the atoll. Many coral scientists remember 1998 as a pivotal moment globally as there was a major ocean warming event. Being on a remote atoll in the middle of the Indian Ocean with little communication with the outside world, I found out about the bleaching by going out for a dive one day and seeing a world of white. I remember diving through a channel connecting the inside to the outside of the atoll and everything was bleached to a depth of at least 30 meters. Corals are animals that grow together in colonies that have distinctive shapes based on the way the individual coral polyps form a calcium carbonate skeleton "cup" around themselves. The animal has a thin layer of tissue over the skeleton and is connected to others through a very thin layer of flesh. Algae species, called zooxanthellae, live in that flesh layer photosynthesizing. They are thus taking in the sunlight and enjoying the protection and access to sunlight afforded by the coral structures and they in turn pass on food they have made to the coral animals. It is an amazing symbiosis – when it isn't too hot! As temperatures get above a certain level, dependent on the species and location, those algae work too hard and start to produce too much of a good thing -all chemical reactions happen faster at higher temperatures. The corals expel the algae, leaving behind a clear layer of flesh and the underlying white skeleton can be seen easily. Sometimes they recover and other times they die off. This is a growing problem in a warming sea, but there is some hope as we have seen, for example, in our work in Kenya that some species have adapted to the higher temperatures. It remains to be seen how destructive this will be for coral reefs in the coming century.

So all was exciting, we had planned on being in Maldives for a long time and I had great funding, access to a boat, and SCUBA equipment. We were learning the language, and I could write notes to my field assistants in Maldivian underwater in a script written right to left in completely previously unrecognizable characters. We had friends and enjoyed a challenging, but very fulfilling life. Then the police knocked on our door.

We were up in the capital of the country to take some time in a place where we could get some ice cream and sit in the a/c reading. The police were not looking for us, but for our friends who were out of the country. Several expats lived in the Maldives who, like us, hoped to live out our lives with our friends and share the hope we had found in our faith. Our passports were taken, and we were confined to that island and repeatedly brought in to the police for questioning. At times we would see our Maldivian friends in the police station as many had been arrested as well. They let us know that they were being beaten and this helped us to mobilize global support for them eventually. We were not allowed to go back to our island and brave friends brought some of our most precious things up to the capital for us as we were then told that we needed to leave the country for good. It was quite an unpleasant experience and still under certain circumstances, I feel the impact of those days on my emotions and decisions.

India

We didn't end up in India by choice. At first, it was quite a struggle to love India, but we did get there. People would often ask us when back in the USA how it was in India, and it is difficult to describe and it is tough to not write in cliches. So, I want to focus on, as you might expect, the ocean. Travelers to India usually focus on the people and the food or if they speak of the wildlife, they mainly think of elephants or tigers. Ironically, A Rocha India's work does focus on elephants and tigers – though we are starting a marine project in 2024.

We moved to the southern tip in a city called Thiruvananthapuram which is the capital of Kerala. This state is known for its lush greenery, good health indices, and being the first freely elected communist government. During our years there the government changed several times, but it was very interesting to try and get our heads around Indian politics – something I am sure we really didn't understand. Culturally it remains that working with your hands or out in the forest or ocean is considered a demeaning occupation. The caste system was still strong and as we would drive to the beach, we saw old ladies sitting on the side of the road under woven palm branch shade breaking large rocks into small ones so that the highway could be made. That was their lot in life – no way up or out except death and then to repeat the cycle according to many beliefs. It was also jarring to go to the local stores and see all the whitening creams designed to make beautiful dark skin whiter. Someone who was lighter skinned was more beautiful by cultural definition. This also made it difficult for young scientists, particularly women, to work in the ocean. One of the most famous Indian coral biologists didn't swim – he had lower-caste young men dive to the bottom and collect corals for him to examine in the laboratory.

This played out as I began to develop a coral reef research program. No scientists had spent any time underwater on the west coast of India and in fact, there was only, at that time in 1999/2000 one dive shop on the Indian subcontinent and that was a 36-hour train ride north in Goa. Dr. John Randall, perhaps the foremost tropical ichthyologist of our time spent a few days looking at the fish, but no systematic study of the reefs had been completed. We received a grant from the National Geographic Society to do just this.

There were three main problems to solve to complete the work: permission from the Indian government, the equipment (mainly air tanks) to do the diving, and someone to work with underwater. Through a series of events now forgotten, I was put in touch with Dr. S Lazarus who was an eminent scientist in the area retiring and wanted to start up an NGO. We began a partnership that lasted the entire time in India and was a great partnership. The closest dive center was in Goa so we needed to import SCUBA cylinders and purchase a dive compressor and dive equipment. Thankfully the NGS grant paid for this including money to have someone get SCUBA certified. My friend Suneesh Thomas was and is an adventurer and was well up for trying it. We got along very well, and he loved the water. He was not a scientist, but as mentioned above, finding one that really wanted to be in the water was often difficult. We traveled to Goa and began a partnership with Barracuda Diving there making friends with the dive shop owners Venkat and Karen Charloo. These initial relationships were significant in all that happened in the ocean over the many years we were there in India 1999-2005.

The trip to Goa was, as always the case for Indian rail travel, interesting. Bobby was very young, less than 1 year old, and traveling north for the long journey. We slept in bunk beds with Cindy cradling Bobby on the inside of the bed so he wouldn't fall onto the floor at night. Food on these trains is amazing – though we were told to always go for the vegetarian option, which we faithfully did. The only time I ever was ill from food in India – and we ate a lot of street food and in some very remote and dicey from a cleanliness perspective situations – was at Pizza Hut in Delhi. I guess I was too comfortable in the western surroundings and ordered a soda, which of course was a mix of water and syrup. That was unpleasant. Goa was a real culinary and cultural difference from Kerala. Tourism is very common in Goa and until relatively recently it was still a Portuguese colony. Barracuda Diving is located in a swanky hotel and though we couldn't afford to stay in it, Venkat arranged for Cindy and Bobby to be able to use the infinity pool and restaurant/bakery while Suneesh and I were out diving.

Our initial work was near to where we were living in Kerala and was very exploratory in nature. We would need to find fishing boats that we could pay to take us out and often just drop down where they said there were rocks to see what was there. The boats were usually small and often had the remnants of the last fishing excursion in the bowels of the boat. This meant for a smelly adventure. But we were exploring, diving where no one had ever gone, and recording for the first time fish species never documented previously. The southern areas of India are heavily influenced by rivers and the geology of the area is mountainous and part of the continental plate, rather than the coral-formed islands of the Maldives. So, if you have ever been in a rocky intertidal zone along the coast where granite boulders are covered with anemones or other small creatures you have an idea of what these "reefs" looked like – just submerged and with a few more sponges and soft corals. The coral percent cover was at about 1% and mostly encrusting forms. The fish life was not as diverse as the Maldives, but being in the tropics was made up of many fish species you would see on a coral reef, including a species of grouper that is only found along the coastal regions of South Asia.

Through Dr. Lazarus, I came into contact, friendship, and eventual collaboration with a remarkable woman named Anita Mary George. She had done her master's degree on soft corals primarily by walking along beaches and picking up dried specimens that washed up. Soft corals are related to hard corals that make coral reefs, but their anatomy is slightly different, and they do not make calcium carbonate skeletons but have flesh that is strengthened with spicules. These are tiny pieces of calcium carbonate or silica that have a characteristic shape depending on the species. It can be possible to identify a soft coral just by looking at the colony as many have distinctive shapes and sizes – the small polyps growing together to form a larger structure. But often you must take a sample back to the lab to dissolve the flesh and spend long hours over the microscope to be able to identify the species. Then there is lots of disagreement and redescriptions of these species so the taxonomy is often changing. To be a soft coral taxonomic expert is challenging indeed. But that is what Anita wanted to become and more so, she wanted to be able to study and collect these species underwater. The problem was, she could not swim and, alas since this was India, her gender also made this nigh-on impossible.

However, Anita was determined. Her parents also were supportive which is quite amazing given the cultural barriers mentioned previously. We went to a local swimming pool nearby where Cindy and I lived and she began to learn basic swimming skills. Then Anita progressed to snorkeling in the swimming pool and eventually snorkeling out in the ocean. There were some shallow areas and a small port with a seawall that had interesting features and for the first time, she could see one of her specimens underwater. We received more funding and we were able to travel again to Goa for dive certification – Venkat's dive shop being the only one on the Indian subcontinent. There is now a dive shop in Thiruvananthapuram and a few others scattered across the country with the majority still in the Andaman and Nicobar Islands. Suneesh had moved on to other adventures so Anita became my dive buddy and we searched the west coast of India to see what we could find.

On one memorable occasion, we were almost at the very southern tip of India diving on a deep rocky area. We worked out of a fishing village and the small boat was stinking of fish as usual. The waves were just at the edge of safety in terms of being able to get in and out of the boat – no ladders or dive platforms – and I was not feeling very well. Most marine biologists still get seasick, and as I don't spend long times out on the water I do as well. One of the things you learn is that you always feel better in the water, well under the water. I had jumped in quickly and with a lot more experience at this point was able to do that on the small rocking boat. Anita took a little longer and as I hung on to the anchor line, I could feel the bile rising in my throat. She jumped in and we started down and I thought I had it beat. It isn't a fun thing to throw up underwater! Imagine the diving regulator that usually guides your gentle exhale of air out into the water leaving that tell-tale sign of diver bubbles. Now imagine vomit going out the same way. The fish enjoyed it, but it was not a pleasant experience. It can be dangerous because of course you must suck in air to keep breathing – so out with the vomit and try to get clean air in through the regulator that was just full of last night's dinner. Thankfully I had enough sense to just go with it and could eventually pull the regulator out of my mouth and rinse it in the seawater and then continue the dive with a burning throat and a bad taste in my mouth.

Venkat at Barracuda Diving and his partner Karen were both keen conservationists eager to take care of the reef and always diving responsibly. They supported our work and gave us access to diving off of Grand Island near the shop and also a bit farther south at Netrani. We in turn were able to describe the reefs and flora/fauna for the first time in the scientific literature.

Venakat was a bit chagrined when we explained that yes, we had to chisel off a few small pieces of coral to take back and identify under the microscope. This is not the mass collection of the Victorian age now on display at museums, but just enough to be able to determine the differences between two closely related species and some tissue for microscopic spicule identification of soft corals and sponges. The latter is an even more primitive animal that has a spicule structure supporting the many interesting shapes from huge barrels, to organ pipes, to an encrusting film.

We went on to publish a number of papers describing the species and reefs we observed. There were a number of first records for India – not new species to science, but species that had never been reported in the scientific literature as occurring in India. We documented the rocky reefs and how much coral, sponge, algae, and other bottom-dwelling species there were in terms of percent cover. Anita published a number of papers on which I was a coauthor which documented the sponge and soft coral species from southern India. All in all, we were able to pioneer marine ecology in many areas and help others understand the wealth of underwater life in India.

The events of the Boxing Day tsunami were devastating across the region and even at many sites where we were working. However, it eventually resulted in a memorable trip to Minicoy, part of the Lakshadweep Island chain, and the expansion of Indian underwater research. There was much money flowing into the area from churches and other international organizations, and most of it was used well. We benefitted from some church funding to develop a bigger marine research team that could look into the impacts of the tsunami on the Indian underwater coastline and its possible effects on fishing communities. This funded another trip up to Goa where several young Indian scientists were trained to dive and eventually trained to do underwater research. Several now continue to do excellent research at universities and research institutions in India. Goa was almost as different a country to these young men as it would have been to travel overseas. They grew up in small towns in very conservative, rural Tamil Nadu and had not traveled much within India. Seeing Indian women ride motorcycles and the changes in food and behavior that is one of the legacies of both extensive tourism and the Portuguese in Goa was at times jarring. It is often good to remember that just because someone has the same passport as you do, they may be as different culturally as someone from a far distant country or perhaps even more different.

Our family was on the beach on Christmas Day 2004 playing in areas that would be slammed with refractive waves from the Boxing Day tsunami which started in Sumatra. We often went to Kovalam Beach which was about a half hour from our home. This was a place that had been the center of the hippie travel movement in the 70s, so I am told, and there had sprung up many beachside small restaurants that still had some degree of foreign tourism, but which mainly now brought Indian tourists. It did seem that they all came to watch our kids play on the beach! We often on a weekend might have a gaggle of tourists taking pictures of our kids playing in the titanium-laced dark sand. There was a Swiss Bakery that had a more Western-style breakfast and our Saturday morning we were often found there enjoying fusion food unavailable in the city. We woke up the next morning to the news that the tsunami had caused extensive damage across the Indian Ocean. I had been scheduled to be underwater the next day and our research trip was promptly canceled.

A tsunami is a huge propagating wave of energy flowing through seawater which reacts differently depending on the geography of a specific location. So, if you were on a boat in the middle of the ocean a huge tsunami wave might feel like a gentle ripple in the water raising and lowering the boat. The Maldives are a bit like a comb in the middle of the ocean in the sense that the islands have developed around an old volcanic ridge and so the wave went through the country never reaching more than a meter or two in height, but since most of the country is less than 2 meters above sea level, there was a time when most of the country was underwater as a strong wave and water ran through villages. About 100 people died in Maldives partly because of this difference in geography. There were in fact divers in the water at the time and they reported strange currents, but no deaths or impact to them. The water simply flowed through the country. So those that died were often the old, infirm, or babies that couldn't hold on to a tree and resist the water flow. However, when the wave hits a continental shelf, it is basically like a ramp letting the wave energy build into a massive wave. The southeast coast of India was hit directly, and many places were destroyed. The wave energy refracted around the southern tip and many westward-facing beach communities were also destroyed, particularly if they were in lower-lying areas. Kovalam beach has quite a steep slope so the wave did some damage and would have swept us out to sea had we been on the beach that day but didn't have the extensive damage like other locations. We waited with our Maldivian friends to hear news of family and friends in the country and over the next several days mourned with many as almost everyone knew at least one person killed, despite the low total number, such are the connections within that country.

The ridge that the Maldives island chain sits on top of extends further north and south. The northern end is called Lakshadweep and is part of India. However, the southernmost island of Lakshadweep is culturally Maldivian and called Minicoy. We had always wanted to visit this place. How different was it from the Maldives? Many people from Minicoy had settled on the west coast of India, particularly in Cochin which was about a 5-hour drive north of our city. Previously I had wanted to do projects in Minicoy particularly and Lakshadweep generally and had even flown up to New Delhi to meet with officials to gain the needed permission. In the end, Anita met a government official and we went through local channels to obtain permission to do work there. I had wanted a good test for the newly formed Reef Research Team and this was it. Anita, now Dr Anita Mary George, led the scientific work and the young men had many dives under their belt. Yet it was usually I who ended up directing things and still was functionally in charge. The idea was that by the end of the trip, the team would be on their own conducting research thus passing the baton on to my Indian colleagues. This is one of the goals of development – they would then have the skills, equipment, training, and desire to continue the project after my absence. We had by then decided that we were going to move to England and so it was particularly important at this juncture.

Cindy and the kids would come along as well on this adventure. Bobby was 5, Sarah was still 3, and Heather was 2. Many people feel they cannot travel with small kids – it can be challenging, but probably not as challenging as taking three small kids to Minicoy! This island is located over 200 miles offshore of India and requires first getting all of our equipment up to Cochin for the 18-hour ferry ride. We did splurge and have a cabin rather than sit out in a common area in chairs or on the floor. However, something in the seasick medicine impacted Cindy in a strange way and we needed to call on the ship's doctor. It turned out fine, but a scare, nonetheless. The kids did well on their adventure, and I remember distinctly our arrival on the island. The ferry could not come directly to the port but needed to stay offshore and outside the atoll lagoon due to the shallow lagoon depth. Everything on the boat was transferred by hand to a waiting local small boat similar to those used in the Maldives. I remember handing Heather at 2 years old over the side of a boat to a waiting stranger and looking down into the several thousand-foot-deep water and hoping not to drop her! We motored into the harbor and it was like being back in Maldives. We put all our things into what is locally known to Maldivians as a corali or elsewhere as tuk-tuks or tri-shaws: a small three-wheeled motorcycle with a shell around it. A corali is the stage of the coconut where the inside meat has dried enough to come loose from the outer husk and rattles around in it loudly. The idea is that you are like that coconut meat rattling around in the small tri-shaw. We stayed at a government housing compound for science and official guests. Basic, but great for setting up our dive compressor and drying wet equipment.

Having been mostly diving the rocky reefs of the west coast of India, the change to a coral reef atoll with low fishing pressure was quite astonishing. We began by working in the lagoon which was a maze of coral. The kids and Cindy could come along at some of the sites with Bobby snorkeling along with us. We would walk in the rich shallow areas looking for invertebrates and watching the fish dart in and out among the coral heads. It was everything you imagine a tropical coral reef to be including the backdrop of white sand beaches lined with coconut palm trees. One memorable find included Bobby picking up a fireworm. These are marine worms, distant relatives of earthworms, but which have tiny, very sharp silica spines in rows along the side and sometimes along the top of their bodies. We ended up spending a very long time with tweezers picking out these spines from his hands. The real treat came in getting out through the channel into the deeper areas which dropped from the surface to thousands of feet below. We dove down the wall as deep as we dared seeing many old friends that preferred the crystal-clear water and coral to the murky, rocky reefs of India's coast.

In the evenings we were often invited to homes for meals and people were intrigued that we knew their language, at least to a passable level. One of the things we were interested in testing was whether some of the radio programs that were being developed for Maldivian followers of Christ were reaching those shores. We had brought a radio to listen in and found that we could hear it just fine. There were also internet resources developed especially to translate the Bible into Dhivehi and we went into an internet café to find the sites. They were blocked in Maldives, but we found that we could access them in Minicoy just fine. Banning books and information never works. Every time the Maldivian government banned a book or website it just increased the curiosity. Everyone should be able to believe as they feel they ought to in their own minds and that is a basic human right often taken away either by governments or cultures. Many Christian groups do this also; discouraging, warning, or punishing those who seek out answers to important questions. Often then when given the chance and finding out that they had been duped into believing lies about that information, people decide to leave those groups. It is no wonder.

The trip ended in a great success. On one of the last days I woke up and went off to a tea shop to enjoy my day around the island. The Reef Research Team had filled their tanks, developed their plan, went out and collected important information on never-before studied reefs, and then returned home safely. Many of those researchers continue to this day to use those skills to study and protect Indian coral reefs. Dr Anita works on soft corals and sponges and has collaborated on projects all over the world including being on a Fullbright Fellowship in the USA at a prominent university traveling to many spots over the country and giving lectures. I am very proud, especially of her, but also grateful for the years of friendship and experiences with my Indian colleagues. We may even begin working again together soon on A Rocha India's first marine project.

I am reminded of an experience we had in India with our Maldivian friends. We were picked up early one morning in a small bus – all twenty or so of us and I think just Bobby, so he must have been only 1 year old at the time. The Hindi music was loud and everyone was talkative all in Dhivehi. We were going on a road trip to the hill country. This was a common affair as we had gone to water parks with them and spent many a day in their home and they in ours. The hill country of Kerala is much cooler than the coast and has beautiful mountains often with waterfalls. We stopped along the way at a roadside area with lots of stalls, crowds, and car traffic. As we exited the bus, I saw a path through the woods off to our left and then to our right the crowds and noise where all our Maldivian friends were heading. Cindy and I looked at each other and headed left! Within minutes we were in a beautiful jungle along a path that we alone were walking. The quiet and beauty were amazing – of course, I don't think we thought about the fact that there were probably tigers back there, but still. For me, it illustrates the principle that Walden made famous, but really harkens back to Jesus' own words (and likely before that) about taking the narrow path rather than the wide one, the high road rather than the low road. Our path has been winding and not always easy but has been full of adventure and interesting people and places because we have often chosen the narrow path.

A global tour of cleaning stations

I flew into Sanaa in Yemen from India not knowing what to expect, having spent very little time in the Middle East. We had a few layovers to and from India for a day in various countries: the UAE, Qatar, and Bahrain. Yemen is the poorer cousin to them all and is often war-torn. I had a growing desire to utilize my science more directly and was exploring that by visiting a colleague Dennis Cox whom I had met elsewhere. He ran a great relief and development program there and had spent much of his life in that area. We drove down to the coast accompanied by an army vehicle, ostensibly to protect us from harm, dropping from the capital city at almost a mile and half of altitude to sea level and the Red Sea. I had never been before and was very excited to get in the water. The army again insisted on sending a guard with us, machine gun and all, though it was likely that they were endangering us more as they were an even more highly desired target. I could only spend a few hours underwater, but it was such a beautiful place and I was able to find my quarry – *Labroides dimidiatus*, the cleaner wrasse.

If you have snorkeled or dove on coral reefs you may have witnessed a curious sight. Normally, a large predatory fish swimming through a school of small potentially edible fish or near a crustacean such as a crab or shrimp causes those animals to scatter or hide. Perhaps think of a drone video you may have seen of a large shark swimming through a school of bait fish – there is a noticeable ring of clear water around the shark that moves with it. The fish are moving out of its way and trying not to be made into a meal. Yet if you look closely, sometimes these large fish stop in a certain area of a coral reef and rather than small fish or crustaceans swimming away, certain species swim closer and in fact sometimes swim right into the large fish's mouth! This is called a cleaning symbiosis and the locations on reefs are called cleaning stations. If you watch the whole encounter, you will see that the large fish swims slowly up to a certain point, opens its mouth, and waits patiently. Often the cleaner fish will do what might be called a little dance – signaling its intentions to the larger fish, effectively saying "Hey, don't eat me, I want to help you." The cleaner fish will go over the large fish's body, removing dead skin, and any parasites, and even swimming into its large mouth and doing the same. The small fish gets some food, and the large fish leaves healthier and there is some indication that the process is actually enjoyable for the larger fish.

A wide range of animals do this, both in and out of the ocean. Think of the oxpecker bird and rhinos on land, for example. Within the sea, many species of fish and a group of shrimp enter into these relationships with many fish species. Some of the cleaner shrimp live in certain areas under rock overhangs and wave their long antennae signaling their presence. If you move slowly you can often offer a hand and get a bit of a manicure underwater. Even large, open-water species such as massive manta rays and schools of hammerhead sharks will travel to particular remote coral areas that reach near the surface of the ocean and offer themselves for cleaning. We often hear about "nature red in tooth and claw" but it is becoming increasingly clear that cooperation and symbiosis have played as much of a role in shaping the world as competition. Maybe we liked the story of competition better since it allows us to live in certain ways that may be to our individual advantage.

My first foray into studying these relationships was in the Bahamas where I spent six weeks in the Exuma Cays Land and Sea Park (detailed in other chapters) studying grouper behavior. We wanted to find out how these fish were spending their time and the role of cleaning stations in impacting their movement and behavior. We mapped out an area of coral reef into grids and knew the location of a cleaning station in the area. We watched the fish to see what they did and where they did it, then removed the cleaning station to see if that changed anything – it did. The fish spent less time in that area and their behavior changed as a result. Just a simple test, but a step towards understanding the wider impact of these stations on fish behavior and movement patterns. It did mean I got to spend a lot of time watching a few individual fish and seeing how much they really did value these cleaning stations.

The next adventure learning about cleaner wrasse was on a trip to Thailand. We had a long-term visa to India but had to leave the country every six months. We often went to Thailand, Sri Lanka, or Malaysia as they were relatively close and relatively inexpensive. Southern Thailand has some amazing reefs and we travelled to Phuket where I was excited to dive. The divemaster who I hired as a dive buddy was excited to be with me since he usually had a gaggle of tourist divers to lead around the reef and couldn't take a lot of time to just sit and watch. The methodology was simply to observe an individual cleaner wrasse for 15 minutes and count and record the number of seconds that it spent cleaning and which species it was cleaning. You might end up with a record of 10 different fish species which the cleaner wrasse had spent cleaning for a certain amount of seconds on average. We tried to survey at least four individual cleaner wrasse and this method I also repeated in Yemen and in India. This provided significant time to just watch, and I highly recommend this to those wanting to go into the field of marine biology. New technology is really helping us to do bigger and more complex work than we could ever have done before – but you still need to understand the places and the species. Sometimes people come up with explanations for their technological results and you can tell they have never or rarely spent any time on a coral reef or watching a particular species. Time in the water is precious!

And what to do about the mimic cleaner wrasse? This species looks virtually identical to the real thing except for the two large fangs. This species wiggles the same way as the real thing, the large fish stops and expects to be cleaned like it's the real thing, and then next thing you know, a chunk of scale, flesh, or gill is taken. At one point I would have tried to explain this in light of the fall of humanity and that this must not have been a part of the original plan. However, these species were doing this, as best we can tell from the fossil record, long before humans came to be. I had always interpreted, or really been told, that death entering the world in the Genesis stories was a physical death. Biology and ecology made a whole lot more sense when I began to interact with Christian theologians who showed very persuasively that this is not necessarily the case. It makes a lot more sense theologically to read those passages of Scripture in a different way and that what is being talked about is the separation between humans and God. Similarly, I had always interpreted, or really been told, that the word "good" in Genesis 1 meant "perfect." Again, as I began to interact with a wider range of Christian theologians I learned that that word could and they would argue should mean something more like "fit for purpose." God made a world that seems to need death to be creative. It doesn't fit with what we might hope for in a God, but if it is a better explanation of reality and is consistent with the Scriptures, not what we hope they say, then we need to accept that and love God for who He is not what we wish Him to be. Perhaps we are all a little more like Voldemort than we would like, assuming death is the worst possible thing that can happen to us.

Rural Oxfordshire, England

Lewknor is a small English village about halfway between London and Oxford. We found ourselves living nearby and not well acquainted with the use of Lewknor church in the opening sequences of the Vicar of Dibley, a beloved BBC drama. My first introduction to a new way of understanding my encounter with that barracuda in the Bahamas came through volunteering in the growing A Rocha UK Chiltern Gateway Project. The children were small, Matthew only two months old when we arrived in England to stay and the others in nursery or primary (elementary) school in the local village of Chinnor. If you look at these places on a map, you can see that though Great Britain is an island, our village is about as far from the sea as one can get. This made it impractical to get involved in marine conservation issues, at least initially. Thankfully A Rocha UK was starting its second conservation site after its wildly successful transformation of the urban Minet Park in London.

The local vicar in Lewknor was Simon Brignall. He was/is a third-order Franciscan, which though at the time this meant nothing to me, and he significantly impacted my thoughts and actions. Simon had also spent significant time in South America, and we resonated together, not totally fitting in with English village culture and life. A small team began to form, including Jo Whitfield, a talented actress and creative, and members from the Oxford Christian Environmental Group SAGE that Martin and Margot Hodson led – another set of relationships that was to have a significant impact on my life.

The first book I remember reading on a faith-based approach to environmental issues was by the Hodsons entitled "Cherishing the Earth". Amazingly, when the second edition was released a few years later, I had a very small part in it, telling the story of A Rocha's marine work in Kenya. I read the first edition during a trip to Australia attending a Lausanne Christian Researchers meeting where I spent a few days exploring Tasmania on my own. Coming back to the youth hostel after a day of spotting wildlife and hiking, it was enthralling to read their book and be challenged that creation care was not an optional extra, but an essential part of my faith.

Dave Bookless featured significantly in this story as well, and I especially remember one project we worked on together, possibly our first meeting and discussions. A Rocha UK had found some funding to gather inner-city Londoners, particularly from South Asian backgrounds, and spend time in Lewknor experiencing the local Aston Rowant National Nature Reserve. Local kids and the kids from London would create art together which would result from time together on the reserve and be displayed in the church. Much of my life to that point had focused on how to help those who don't profess Christian faith to learn in their own context and culture how they might do that. Long discussions with Dave about the role and place of what many term evangelism in the context of creation care ensued. This was one of several cracks in the façade of American cultural Christianity that was forming in my life. While A Rocha is explicitly Christian in its approach to conservation and does not shy away from conversations about how to follow Christ during environmental care, the emphasis on creation care for its own sake – or really God's sake – is clear.

Some say that in particularly conservative Christian churches, the Bible starts at Genesis chapter 3. This is the story of the Fall when Adam and Eve choose to disobey God. Otherwise, Genesis 1 is often looked at to combat perceived scientific hegemony. However, I began to discover a much richer and more extensive theology based on the first two chapters of Genesis. At this point in the story, though, it was the focus of that first chapter on God declaring His creation good that took hold of my mind. I thought, as has often been quoted to me erroneously, that after repeated declarations of the non-human parts of creation good, God finally gets to the best bit, us, and declares us very good. Yet if you look at the text, what it says is that He looked at ALL he had made and declared it very good.

It was the completion of creation that was "better" so to speak –
using the modifier very. Yet, all creation was valuable to God
and declared good, before humans were created. What I learned
during this time was the idea that many call the intrinsic value
of creation. There is a bit of tricky wordsmithing here which we
may get into at some point since technically the Bible is saying
that creation has value because of God's declaration of
goodness. Be that as it may, the main point for me was that the
non-human creation has goodness and worth without regard to
how or if humans value it.

One of the ways we tried to pass on this and other thoughts
about caring for creation was through a nature club at Lewknor
C of E Primary School. Weekly after-school activities and
teaching allowed me to delve into various species and habitats,
particularly local or national (UK) ones that I was unfamiliar
with. We thought about hedgerows, so ubiquitous in that part
of England, and the recently re-introduced red kites, thriving
after removing persecution for perceived impacts on livestock. I
kept reptiles as a work colleague leaving the country
bequeathed his collection of boa constrictors to me. These
became stars of the show as the kids were able to hold and learn
about snakes.

The growing Chiltern Gateway Project also began to volunteer
and collaborate with the Aston Rowant National Nature
Reserve nearby, managed by Natural England. This is chalk
country, and the geology is essentially marine. Long ago when
the UK was underwater and more tropical in temperature, giant
ichthyosaurs and other marine dinosaurs roamed the waters.
Dinoflagellates are small single-celled algae that have a calcium
carbonate "shell" around them. They swarm in the trillions and
when they die, they sink to the bottom, their calcium adding to
a growing layer which under pressure becomes limestone and
chalk. This provides a type of habitat and soil profile that
houses different species and ecosystems. This includes rare
butterflies and a species of ant called the yellow meadow ant.

One of the first and only terrestrial studies that I have participated in was here at the Aston Rowant National Nature Reserve. Juniper trees are important in northern climes most notably used in the production of gin. Land use changes and climate were impacting the abundance and health of juniper trees and the Aston Rowant National Nature Reserve was identified as a location for active restoration. We also needed to know how many and where the trees were on the reserve so I participated in a weeklong study mapping the juniper. We would identify a particular tree, record biological characteristics, and then record its position using a GPS. The resulting report provided a baseline to judge future activities.

The restoration work involved planting juniper trees. A Rocha wanted to involve the church in this and so began several events where local church members put on their wellies, hiked into the reserve, and worked with reserve staff to plant fields of small juniper trees. Our children were young, but they joyfully grabbed a small tree, dug a hole, planted it, and wrote their name on the stake holding it up. Over the years we have gone back and tried to find "their" trees. We have a general idea now, their names long weathered off the stakes. But it is such a joy to visit those places and see the tangible results of our work. This began a long partnership with the nature reserve staff for events where A Rocha became a trusted partner locally, even at times being called in at the last minute to run an event if Reserve staff fell ill or otherwise couldn't lead.

A Rocha values cooperation with local groups, whether faith-based or not. It is one of our core values. This time of working with the local school, church, Nature Reserve, and other civic groups set me on a good path for my future marine work. Collaboration is so important and often the church wants to do its own thing. Another collaborator and hugely influential place in my life at this time was Hilfield Priory.

Our small team in Lewknor decided to take a retreat to Hilfield. This is a group of Anglican Franciscan brothers who live in community and have an emphasis on peace, justice, and the environment. They have a monastery on the south coast of England that hosts groups and leads retreats in and amongst the daily work and worship of the brothers. Up until my time in the UK, I would have resisted and rejected most formal types of religion. I had no interest in tradition nor any experience in liturgical forms of church. I jumped in locally in our village joining the ministry team of our Church of England Parrish, mostly taking on preaching a few times a month. The Catholic orders of Franciscans, Dominicans, Jesuits, and Benedictines feature more prominently in my story later, but this was my first introduction, and I really grew in my faith through these forms that were so foreign. I find that I struggle with prayer but can pray for long periods of time when led through the liturgy. I find it ironic that I once criticized these dead traditional ways as unscriptural, but then found out in actuality we read more scripture in one of these liturgical services than in months of those from churches I had attended to that point.

For many reasons, the work in Lewknor itself began to come to an end and we had added several folks to the team from the village where we lived, particularly our very close friends the Swaffields. Ian took on a leadership position and was always a driving force of activity. Shane always creatively helping us to communicate through art, crafts, and practical projects. Our families worked together volunteering and spending much time in and around the Chiltern Hills that surrounded Chinnor. We began to experiment at our local church with integrative services and weekend events. One memorable weekend saw the Bat Conservation Trust giving a talk called Bats in the Belfry at the church and then going out to listen for bats in the churchyard. Moths were trapped and passed around during the Sunday service while recorded bat sounds played all the while linking this to our faithful practice of the Christian faith. We began to do larger events such as Chinnor Goes Wild where we camped and held weekend weekend-long series of activities inviting the whole village to participate.

The time spent with A Rocha UK living out this new integrated life and experimenting with how my Christian faith could find its expression locally was hugely formative in putting together my past and moving me towards a different vision of the future. Alongside this practical outworking of my learning was the intellectual formation happening through the amazing banquet that is the British science and faith community.

United Kingdom

I began to speak more locally about marine conservation issues. I remember giving a sermon in Dorchester Abbey, a large church nearby where one of our bishops presided. I was licensed to preach in our Parish of four local churches and did so at least once a month for many years. I don't remember the exact occasion but was asked to speak on the ocean. As was often the case when speaking to people in this part of the country, I started by reminding them they lived on an island. Google Maps is great for this, staring at a local level where all is farmland and houses and then zooming out to show the British Isles. I look back now at my basic and clumsy attempts to integrate conservation and faith in speaking and writing and wince. But it was an important time for me to integrate a life of learning about my faith with a life of learning about the ocean and marine conservation.

In all English villages, there is a village hall. This is a place that local groups can use for activities and almost always has a kitchen. The Mother's Union is one such group that uses these village halls for events, gathering women to connect on particular issues. I spoke to many of these groups around our local area and I often started talks by showing pictures of fantastic marine creatures, usually as a geeky scientist, starting from the least complex such as jellyfish, and rising up the taxonomic spectrum eventually to marine mammals such as seal and orcas. I would then ask them where they needed to go to see these amazing animals and often the answer was some far-off tropical country. The punch line was, of course, that the photos were all taken around Great Britain. There is such a beauty and wealth of wildlife in northern places – it just takes some fortitude to see them.

One of my first forays into snorkeling in the UK I thought I had killed my son! Bobby was about 5 at the time and he had grown up in India in the tropics. He loved the water and I decided to go away with him to the south coast to explore for fossils and look for seahorses that reside in the area. We learned about the walking path system in the UK, traipsing through private property legally if you stay on the path. In this case, it was a Ministry of Defense bombing range! No bombs fell, but some very curious horses bothered us enough as we picnicked that we had to flee. We stayed in a Youth Hostel near Lulworth Cove, famous for its arch which we also swam out to. Traipsing across the hills and along the coast towards a likely snorkeling area, we jumped in and were enthralled, until I noticed Bobby was so blue that we needed to get out of the water. There was likely no real danger, but it took a very long time for him to warm up. We didn't see any seahorses, but that began a love affair with British beaches that expanded through family trips over the years.

Family holidays were usually spent in a youth hostel somewhere close to the sea. We wanted to see Lundy Island – well, I did anyway. This is the first marine protected area in the UK and is a model of success. It comes as no surprise that if you protect fish and other creatures such as lobster from fishing, they become more abundant, larger, and more diverse. We decided to camp a few nights in a campground on the cliffs facing Lundy. There was a massive storm where rain poured through the tent like a river soaking most of us. One of the poles broke and we spent the next night before the ferry to Lundy at an interesting B&B trying to dry our things. Once we arrived on Lundy Island, we enjoyed game nights in front of the fire and spent the days wandering the island, exploring its tidepools. I often in these days had to make choices between exploring underwater myself or being a part of family activities. I did travel a lot and so had many opportunities to do things that the kids and Cindy could not, so in this case and many others, chose to stick with the family. I don't regret that at all. The family did, though, often find that our holiday sites were located near something to do with A Rocha or some marine thing I wanted to see. In this case, the hope was to snorkel with seals. My older two were nine and eleven years old and good snorkelers. One of the things I tried to do throughout their lives was make sure they always had snorkeling kit and a wetsuit, the latter likely handed down to the younger ones and sometimes ill-fitting. We entered the cold water and swam out with no seals coming close, just popping up their heads some distance away to check us out. I had, without much thought, told the kids to not worry if a seal might grab their fin – they were just playing and curious. Turns out I traumatized my daughter as she kept imagining a massive seal grabbing her fin!

I find that there are ocean people and non-ocean people. Peter and Miranda Harris who co-founded A Rocha were an interesting mix. Much of the beginnings of A Rocha followed Peter's obsession with birds and developed a terrestrial bent, despite Miranda's love of the sea. During a visit to Florida a few years prior to the fateful car accident that took Miranda's life, she and I swam joyfully in the sea, taking her hand to help her through the large waves. Pure joy in her face. Peter was on the beach photographing shorebirds. This isn't a right or wrong or good or bad position. But it does continue to cause me to think that trying to "convert" someone to becoming a sea person is difficult and I need to focus my life and work with people who already get it. Many in A Rocha UK at the time were not ocean people – or at least Dave Bookless was as mad a birder as Peter was and as he was leading the work and also living in urban London, the work didn't flow yet to the sea.

An exception was that A Rocha UK was expanding its work by partnering with landholders and other NGOs throughout the country. One of these was a Christian camp called St Madoc on the far western edge of the Gower Peninsula in Wales. It sits on top of a hill with, importantly, a large beach area nearby. We were going to do a weekend bio blitz and myself and Steve Holloway, a colleague who we were within the Maldives and now also residing in England, joined in on the marine team. About 40 of us in total, mostly terrestrial teams, came for the weekend gathering on a Friday night to hear Rev Dr. John Rodwell speak about Adam as the first taxonomist. We then spent all day Saturday collecting biodiversity information with the moth and bat teams working well into the night. It was such a rich experience – at least in terms of the Christian fellowship and learning more about connecting conservation and faith. The beach was less diverse, but still great to explore. One of our subsequent family holidays sans Cindy who we think was visiting her sister in the US, returned to St Madoc with the kids helping me and Sarah Leedham, former and current ARUK staff, then St Madoc staff, to develop an identified shell collection for environmental education.

I am not much of a taxonomist. Though I could identify most Caribbean fish at one time during my Ph.D., since then, I have always struggled to be able to keep species IDs in my head. I remember at the St Madoc retreat walking the beach with Helen Demopoulus who spent time with A Rocha in Lebanon and was now working with ARUK and she asked me what a particular species of clam was whose shell she had just picked up. I replied "I have no idea" – thoroughly unbothered by my lack of knowledge and continuing our conversation on some abstruse topic, I am sure. Later she and I snorkeled in Kenya at the Watamu site and there at least I could tell most of the families of fish and identify the main groupings of animals. It is an important skill and many in A Rocha have it for their particular group of animals they focus on or more generalists who seem to know everything. Knowing the species is an important skill and critical for conservation. My lack of this skill has not, I think, hindered my ability to achieve conservation – it just means I must pick folks to be a part of my team who know them. Subsequent work in Kenya with now Dr Benjamin Cowburn has confirmed this and he is someone who I have greatly benefitted from partnering with – he is also a lot of fun to be with and we have had many adventures described elsewhere in this book across Asia, Africa, and Europe.

Various other family and work trips around the UK helped us to enjoy our adopted home and contribute to the growing awareness of creation care within local churches. One day we received an email that was to impact much of the rest of our lives. An undergraduate student named Hannah Hereward inquired if she could do her dissertation working in Kenya. We were beginning to develop that program within A Rocha and I was leading their marine work and encouraging young students to volunteer and contribute to conservation there, as detailed in another chapter. As we talked, Hannah invited us to her family home in Cornwall. I politely replied we were a family of six, young kids, etc. and you don't really know what you are suggesting. However, she persisted, and this began a long collaboration and an important friendship with the Hereward family. Cornwall is a bit like the Florida of the USA – overrun by tourists at certain times of the year, with beautiful beaches, but with dramatic cliffs. Over many trips and years, we explored just a small portion of that beautiful part of the world and their family's friendship remains to this day an important part of our lives and story.

Hannah pursued a Masters at the Marine Biological Laboratory – the world's oldest such institution and home to a cadre of globally influential researchers. She was able to lengthen the normal one-year master's into two years and thus spend time as a Marine Researcher with A Rocha including her faith in a conservation project at Lee Abbey, a Christian conservation center on the north Devon coast. This was a productive time of helping Lee Abbey to more fully utilize their small beach for marine education and some of our first experimentations with integrating the ocean into worship experiences.

There remains much to explore along the British coastline – I still have yet to swim with basking sharks, for example. It was hard for a tropical marine biologist to fully appreciate the cold, dark, and many times unclear waters. Yet our many experiences along its coasts and in those cold waters provided much delight.

Oxford and Cambridge Universities United Kingdom

The UK has the advantage of officially being a Christian country. While many in the church see this as a disadvantage in regard to personal faith development and the pervasive cultural Christianity, what it has practically meant from a science and faith perspective is that there has not been the duality seen in places like North America. Christian scientists can openly practice their faith and have thought long and hard about how their faith and scientific practice integrate. This resulted in a rich banquet of resources and relationships to explore.

Two groups, besides A Rocha, which fed my growing interest in an intellectually rigorous approach to my faith which could integrate with a rigorous approach to science were Christians in Science (CiS) and the Faraday Institute. Both groups held a series of lectures, and conferences, and wrote books ranging from general science and faith issues to very specific topics. One of the first CiS conferences I attended was their annual meeting held in Edinburgh which was in conjunction with the Canadian and USA groups of similar interest. This was a rich week of exploring science and faith topics of a broad range and began a journey along a path that would keep digging deeper particularly in the area of conservation science and the ocean.

One of the topics, which I won't delve into deeply here, which is usually a stumbling block for those of us from North America who grew up in conservative Christian churches is, of course, creation and evolution. Thankfully I grew up in a thinking church and family who though they couldn't quite fully embrace evolution, did not preach a dogmatic creationism. There were many barriers to seeing how compatible Christianity is with a scientific view of origins and being in the UK was particularly helpful. I began to see generally how much of what I thought of as my faith and beliefs was actually

American faith and beliefs and probably even more specifically, white, middle-class, midwestern, mostly Reformed Christian faith. Jumping into the ministry team at our local Church of England Parrish in Chinnor taught me how culturally based my assumptions, applications, and interpretations of the Bible actually were. I began to see that my view of origins and any reticence I had about fully accepting the science on this issue were culturally based, not biblically based.

Fully jumping into the science was in many ways like a second conversion to me. The world around me lit up and screamed of God. I began to hear the trees clapping their hands as the Biblical prophet Isaiah puts it or in the even less literal Psalmist's perspective "let the rivers clap their hands." For a few short months, my bodily reaction was one of attunement to the rest of creation and their praises to God. I am learning now how to hear that again and with intentional effort I am beginning to connect in that special way I once did.

This began a time of enchantment with the whole Oxbridge scene. This term refers to Oxford and Cambridge Universities. Many of the lectures were held in ornate halls at either of these universities where we sipped wine and ate cheese after some well-known Christian scientist spoke about their work and faith. I attended events at the Faraday Institute at Cambridge, a group at that time within the university system who were actively researching, writing, and speaking on science and faith issues. I eventually became and remain an Associate of this institute which contributed so much to my deepening integration of science and faith. We stayed in the university halls and dined in Hogwartsesque rooms filled with luscious food, good conversations, and the ubiquitous alcohol found at scientific meetings.

Looking back, my first attempts at writing and presenting on this issue were quite clumsy and I still think that my lack of any formal theological training is probably a hindrance. My work with A Rocha in the UK and then starting in 2010 with A Rocha in Kenya led to opportunities to present an argument for the need to include Christian faith in conservation science. At the time, pre-Laudato Si, there was quite an antagonism to Christianity within the conservation world. Others have written on the historical reasons for this and will not attempt even a summary here. So while anyone entering conservation science these days can see at large scientific meetings and UN conferences a visible Christian component, that was not the case at that time. I began to work more with the international team of A Rocha and initially, this began through a writing project which ended up looking at case studies of several A Rocha projects in the context of biodiversity and poverty. I then attempted to think through some of the issues specific to the ocean and how my own area of study, marine protected areas, related to the Christian faith. This resulted in a Grove Booklet called Hope for the Ocean.

The focus of this booklet was on examining some of the major threats to the ocean and one particular solution that should come as no surprise, marine protected areas (MPAs). I then went on to look at some Biblical resonances with the idea of MPAs such as the Sabbath, justice, and humility. This was part of my journey in learning the difference between trying to use the Bible to prove something and seeing how the Bible resonates with particular concepts and provides evidence for support. It is a subtle but important difference. Alistair McGrath and his voluminous work have been helpful over the years in teasing out this difference.

Around this time I was asked to speak a series of lectures at the London School of Theology on the idea of Biodiversity and Beauty. This began a journey, which I am still on, in trying to understand the place of beauty in conservation and the Christian faith. In one way, it provided a foil for intrinsic value. Yes, we need to protect things simply because God declared them good, even if they are not useful to us or even repugnant to us. However, there is something important about a beautiful creature that also mirrors God's beauty and causes one to delight, wonder, and react with awe at a powerful experience.

On the scientific front, I had a zeal for preaching the idea that the Christian faith had something to offer conservation. Not a new idea, but there was relatively little input within the marine sciences. I gave a talk about A Rocha's work at the World Conference on Marine Biodiversity in Aberdeen Scotland and someone I knew suggested that my talk sounded more like a sermon than a scientific presentation. I gave a short talk at the 1st International Marine Protected Areas Congress in Washington DC where I showed a picture of an angry preacher and suggested that was most scientists' view of Christians, which needed to change. I imagine I was quite irritating. My zeal would eventually temper and become channeled into more thoughtful work with colleagues such as our recent paper examining faith and conservation in the so-called secular west.

The learning process of trying to integrate theology with science has been steep. I am thankful for the integration of thinking that I benefitted from by coming into contact with many British colleagues. I don't think there is a better place to learn about that integration in the world.

The world

Some of my first attempts at linking more traditional Christian mission pursuits with conservation were found in my Grove booklet *Hope for the Ocean*. Looking back, it is fairly embarrassing to read, but part of writing and presenting your ideas to the public is to have them critiqued, even if it is simply from yourself rereading your early thoughts. I mainly argued that how we live daily can beneficially or negatively impact humans and that there is a significant opportunity to bless others through projects in tropical marine biodiversity hotspots. The attempt was to try and put marine biodiversity conservation into the context of the usual foci of Western Christian missions.

Reflecting on a more recent Grove Booklet entitled *Marine Plastics* and though I am sure I will feel the same way in 10 years about it, right now it expresses a more developed view of God's Kingdom and the role of conservation not as a means to an end or an opportunity to slip in Jesus, but as an essential part of our service as followers of Christ.

For much of my life in England, I spent time working with more traditional parachurch agencies and within the Church of England in our Parish. The two sets of people presented two different, but related barriers to integrating conservation with the Christian faith. My work colleagues were focused on how to start new churches and conservation seemed to either not have any relevance or was something that maybe should happen, after the church was started. Those in the church were in many ways involved in conservation or at least environmentalism – recycling, reducing use, etc – but often failed to see how this related to their Christian faith.

Often you must start where people are at and within the frameworks within which they are already thinking. With my work colleagues, I tried along with a few others to show the opportunity for service and for placing new teams in areas that were in desperate environmental crisis. But also began to explore the justice theme from that booklet. Many conservative Christian groups began to understand what might be called social justice. As caring for the physical needs of those they were seeking to meet the spiritual needs of began to increase in importance, it was easy to show how the state of the environment was impacting those they were trying to serve.

Yet this is and continues to be an anthropocentric argument, looking at the environment mainly as a platform for the grand human performance of life. Some of my thoughts on how to shift beyond this and think more in the way of God's whole Kingdom are found in an article directed towards church planters, particularly in areas where there are no churches. I argue in an article published in the International Journal of Frontier Missiology that we need to think more holistically about unreached places rather than just unreached peoples.

I argued in that article that there has been significant theological research and missions practice in the area of creation care which the above overview only gives a brief glimpse. While people group missiology was immensely useful for mission practice, I have argued that it is an incomplete missiology. We have learned much in the past forty-plus years of both studying this topic and putting it into practice. Integral or holistic mission missiology, as well as from groups such as the Fruitful Practices research team, shows us that a focus only on seeing churches started was incomplete and lends itself to an anthropocentric and dualistic Biblical interpretation. The 2010 Cape Town Lausanne meeting helped the global Christian community to see its call for the whole Church to take the whole Gospel to the whole world. Creation care helps us to move towards a theocentric vision of mission with God's glory and kingdom at the center. Far from diminishing the value of reaching unreached people, it helps us to see them as God intended.

My time working on these issues has been made significantly more productive and enjoyable through my long collaboration with Dr David Greenlee. Much of our research and writing together focused on issues other than creation care, but David is an avid birder and loves to discuss ideas, so we found plenty of time to grow together in our understanding of how creation care integrates with other aspects of the Christian faith. His work with Operation Mobilization is broad, but in recent years has helped them to think deeply about how to integrate creation care into all aspects of work, life, and ministry. It was an honor to sit as an outside member of the task force thinking about these issues. One of the areas that we worked on together was the issue of how creation care might integrate with seeing new groups of followers of Jesus form particularly in areas where there were none previously. The focus was more broadly on the role of development in this process and specifically how creation care relates to this nexus. This provided an opportunity to read and think on a very specific issue and to pull in what others have written more generally. I remember needing to move ahead significantly on the article and doing so on a layover in London. I walked the streets and sat in a number of pubs reading and writing. A friend from Orlando had free passes for the London Eye, so I finally was able to ride that large Ferris wheel and contemplate creation care looking out over that massive city with its large green lungs – the parks we love so much. The result is a chapter in a book called Undivided Witness and continues to impact the way mission agencies are seeking to approach their work.

My experience of working ten years in South Asia as a more traditional Christian worker, but with a specific emphasis on helping groups of people follow Jesus, provided a basis for writing with some semblance of authority. Though now, of course, looking back, I think much differently about the process. My short time in Yemen and working in development after the Asian tsunami had broadened my understanding and practice of Kingdom work leaving me desiring to use my science more directly for ministry. My time in England and shifting to work with A Rocha helped me to understand and implement a more fully biblical approach to life and ministry which incorporated serving the cosmos not just one species, to put it grandly. The two papers detailed above allowed me to come full circle and think about the endeavor that our family started out on so long ago. We left what could have been a decently comfortable and enjoyable life in America as a marine biologist and professional musician to serve. The system into which we entered didn't really know what to do with a marine biologist and only valued my skills and desires in so much as they served the main purpose of seeing groups of followers of Jesus form in places where they were not. The mission system is morphing and growing and groups like OM are encouraging us to take professional learning seriously. Increasingly these types of agencies are integrating creation care into their work, some alas continue to use it as another means to an end. But it has been satisfying personally to grow in this way and to be able to be a small part of shifting a larger system to serve God more fully.

Kenya

When you think of Kenya what comes to mind? Probably the Masai Mara and a safari looking for lions or maybe the wildebeest migration. My experience of Kenya is of beautiful beaches and coral reefs. I had heard about A Rocha's work in Kenya during a conference in Germany via some colleagues who worked nearby. They were not Christians and thought of it as a good, but strange mixture of faith and conservation. I was traveling to Kenya for a conference related to my work with churches and did, in fact, visit the Masai Mara with my son Bobby. He was ten at the time and he came along with me for several weeks. We did see cheetahs, lions, etc. But we also decided to visit the coast – a trip that would change the direction of my life and that of our family.

The trip to the coast started memorably – we had our own plane down. Kenyan Airways has small planes that fly to the coast from Nairobi most days and we had booked our flight. When we arrived, we were the only passengers. They debated putting us on a different airline, but in the end, Bobby and I had the plane to ourselves. We landed at Malindi Airport and made our way to Mwamba, A Rocha's center in Watamu about 45 minutes from the airport. We stayed in a room that would become my normal haunt on trips to Mwamba and met Dr. Colin Jackson for the first time. Colin had started the center many years ago and was the National Director for A Rocha Kenya.

Waking up at Mwamba is often easy – the monkeys make it difficult to sleep in. They play on the tin roofs and at times you must guard your breakfast from a cheeky individual looking for a snack. The center is located just off the beach with a 30-second walk down a sand path dumping you onto what is considered one of the most beautiful beaches in East Africa. You can smell the ocean and the tropical flowers. Directly offshore are coral reefs – these are lagoon reefs behind the reef crest of the offshore fringing reefs. Later studies by our team revealed that these reefs only make up 1% of the habitat in this area, but they are the draw that initially pulled me in. We also met Mohamed who was the regular boatman for the center taking people out to see the reefs – he and his family would become friends over the years of visits. Bobby and I were able to spend some good time together and Colin made a startling request. He spoke with me about a small donation that had just been made for marine conservation work and would I take charge of directing how it was used. I agreed, of course, and have been helping to support the work there ever since.

Given that we lived thousands of miles away in the UK and even with traveling to Kenya a few times a year for several years in a row, the majority of work there has been done through others. At the beginning of our time in 2010/2011 this was primarily through experienced interns, volunteers, and students. Much of this was led by Benjamin Cowburn and he and I have worked closely together ever since. Ben loves the ocean and grew up in the UK spending long periods of time at the waterside in Cornwall. He had just graduated from Oxford University and was keen to work in Kenya. He initially volunteered for six months taking on the task of our first project. The Watamu Marine National Park is a relatively small area (10 km²), and the beachfront of the park can be walked in about an hour. The park extends out to the reef crest (so we thought, though that comes later in the story), and the park is mostly relatively shallow water with maximum depths of 8-10 meters in a few places. Much of it can be snorkeled easily and we have mostly used this method to study the park primarily due to costs associated with SCUBA diving.

Watamu is a big tourist destination because of the beaches and Marine National Park. Fishers who could access capital to purchase boats now take tourists out to the reef to snorkel earning more than they might have through fishing. The park is managed by Kenya Wildlife Services (KWS) a government agency tasked with managing all the national parks in the country. All the tourist boats went to one particular reef called

Coral Gardens and the question KWS asked us to answer was whether or not the tourists were damaging this site. Many people want to see coral reefs and all the amazing fish life that is there. When the boat pulls up to the reef fish swarm around it – the legacy of feeding the fish. You can swim through clouds of brightly colored fish and if you search can find eels, rays, and other interesting creatures. Benjo, as we call him, had the enviable or unenviable, depending on your perspective, job of following snorkelers around in the water and determining if they were doing damage.

We found that the reef visited by tourists manifested observable damage and differences in ecological character, which potentially compromised its ecological sustainability. Despite these observations, most tourists did not notice the changes or were happy with their experience and hence the economic sustainability of the park appears secure. However, the future trajectory of reef conditions and tourism on the reef is complex and difficult to predict, which could lead to a trade-off between conservation and income-generating goals.

It is easy to love something to death. A famous paper written by Garrett Hardin called The Tragedy of the Commons spelled this out. Imagine walking through a park and seeing a field of beautiful flowers. No one owns the park, so to speak, it is a commons. Everyone can use it. What does it hurt for you to pick just one flower? The problem is that the thousands of people after you start thinking the same way and eventually the park has very few flowers. This is when another famous concept and paper comes into play by Daniel Pauly who describes the Shifting Baseline Syndrome. If you walked through that park years later with, say 90% of the flowers gone, you might still think it beautiful. After all, much of the rest of your city is concrete, and here is a place with some flowers. You think this is normal for that park and how it should be – your idea of what a healthy, beautiful park has shifted. Some grumpy old guy might tell you something like "You should have seen it when I was a kid" – and they would be right, but that guy probably picked some of those flowers. We get used to the slow decline in beauty of the natural world around us. A study on the amount of weight of mammals on the planet (so that an elephant counts more than a mouse) revealed that only 4% of mammal weight globally is actually wildlife! The remaining 96% are humans and our livestock. We have so altered our planet that it would be unrecognizable to our ancestors.

Does it really matter whether or not it is a cow or an elephant in that field? I think it does. One of the theological principles that captured my imagination was the idea of intrinsic value or the goodness of creation irrespective of its value to humans. In Genesis 1, God declares His creation good before humans are on the scene. Throughout Scripture, creation praises God independently of humanity and the Biblical book Colossians tells us that creation was made by, for, and through Christ and is itself healed through the cross. This was revolutionary to my thinking as a follower of Christ. One of my first forays into trying to express this practically came about because of a report of a dugong being sighted in Kenya. These are large marine mammals – sea cows – and the Indo-Pacific relative of manatees. They have been hunted since humans could do so and have been wiped out through most of their range. A dugong hadn't been spotted in Kenya in a long time – but what was the big deal? I argued that these animals were one voice in the orchestra of creation praising God and that protecting them and helping them thrive again in Kenya was an important part of our Christian faith. If "sea cows" were replaced pound for pound by land cows, it would not be the same. Something in creation would have diminished by the sea cows disappearing and not praising God anymore. Diversity is an important part of how God's world was made.

One of the ways in which we can determine whether a species or habitat is in decline is to monitor specific aspects of populations or habitat characteristics. For example, if you are concerned with the conservation status of corals, you could monitor the percent coverage of coral in a specific place – in this case, how much of the surface space of Coral Gardens reef in Watamu Marine National Park is occupied by corals. Or in a larger sense, how much of this park is occupied by coral reefs. It would have been relatively easy to choose the usual suspects to monitor – fish and corals – since that is often the easiest and the most interesting in terms of activity. It is fun to survey fish and coral populations. It is much harder, though, to survey for other species such as mollusks or crustaceans. It is also a lot more fun to snorkel on a coral reef than over an area of monotonous sand. However, we didn't want to jump right into monitoring. There had been some work already done on a portion of the fish population in Watamu and on the coral reefs. What else was there that might be just as important or perhaps more so?

While this musing about how to understand the marine biodiversity of Kenya was happening, we began to get a lot of interest from young Christian scientists who wanted to come and experience A Rocha's philosophy expressed through our marine conservation work. There remains essentially no other Christian group doing marine conservation – though many are advocating for policy and personal behavior change that would benefit the ocean. A major leap forward in our work came as the result of a power trio of young women: Hannah Hereward, Cassie Raker, and Dorothea Seeger, nee Kohlmeier. Many others came alongside during this time as well including Victoria Sindorf, Tim Gordon, Aline Nussbaumer, Matteus Horions, Benjamin Van Baelenberghe, Jack Kamire, and Dawn Goebbels.

The idea occurred to us to develop a taxon-by-habitat matrix for the park that could be filled in through time with many volunteers and Benjo taking the lead to implement the work. So, I sat in the UK most of the time on Skype with Benjo and the others hearing of their amazing experiences on these reefs and visiting once or twice a year to better understand the progress and that place for myself. This essentially involved documenting all the different types of habitats in the park that were present such as seagrass, coral reefs, sandy bottom, etc. and then we knew the different types of organisms that were likely to be there and listed these as separate groups, usually by

Phylum or other major grouping. This produced a table that allowed us to assign to a volunteer usually a taxonomic group that they would then focus on learning the identification of species and then snorkel in each habitat and determine which species of that taxonomic group was there. Some groups of species are very hard to identify without expert training. So, we still have not assessed groups like sponges or small crustaceans among many others. Lots of work still to do!

Benjo was interested in doing a Ph.D. and was able to secure a place at his undergraduate institution Oxford University. This gave the work some status it might not have had, though it did make Benjo's work difficult at times. There is often a mismatch between a home university in a Western culture that runs on deadlines and non-western cultures that are more event-orientated. Similarly, with grant funding – it can be easy to sit in some office somewhere in the west and wonder why you can't just get out on the reef to get that data – why the delays? Yet there are often many things that cause these delays – such as the usual power outage on Thursdays at Mwamba during this time or needing to secure permission to collect the data from someone who had just left for Nairobi for several weeks. Benjo did amazingly well navigating these pressures and to this day is such a pleasure for me to work with. The work on biodiversity was summarized in a publication in the journal Atoll Research Bulletin.

The group of volunteers and students began to coalesce into a Marine Team. This was somewhat of an advisory panel and served to generate resources for A Rocha on marine conservation. The hope was that this team would help advise others in A Rocha on how to start marine projects and form a group that could help move the work ahead. We memorably gathered a good portion of the team at the Sluka house in Chinnor England over one Thanksgiving. Our small home with one bathroom hosted the six Slukas and seven Marine Team members, including A Rocha Kenya's first Kenyan marine biologist Peter Musembi. We planned and played together in a way that I had envisioned for the team to encourage each member in their personal path while advancing the marine conservation agenda within A Rocha.

There is a curious group of fish called hawkfishes. These occur throughout the world's tropical seas and primarily live on coral reefs. As their name suggests, they perch on suitable pieces of coral and then hunt smaller fish and crustaceans. There are only one species of this family in the Caribbean, and I had often enjoyed seeing the redspotted hawkfish (*Amblycirrhitus* pinos) in my research there. Having always wanted to study these fish and given that there were very few studies from the western Indian Ocean, Hannah Hereward and I embarked on describing their diversity, abundance, and habitat preferences in Watamu Marine National Park. Hannah did most of the fieldwork, but I was able to travel to Watamu during her six months of residence there and help with some of the work. The old adage that correlation does not imply causation is always important to remember in field research. However, one of the ways to begin to understand where an animal lives is to correlate time spent with specific habitat characteristics. You can then begin to use your knowledge of ecology to try and build new hypotheses as to why they are spending more time in those places. These can then be tested by further observation or ideally experimentation. We mainly observed the hawkfish and found species-specific macrohabitat associations, whereby higher densities of arc-eye hawkfish *Paracirrhites arcatus* were found on deep reefs, and higher densities of freckled hawkfish *P. forsteri* were found on shallow reefs. In addition, arc-eye hawkfish showed a positive association with the hard-branching coral *Pocillopora*. However, as there was less *Pocillopora* on the deep reefs, arc-eye hawkfish does not prefer the deep reefs simply because there is more *Pocillopora* present, lending support that these species are facultative coral dwellers. The increased density of hawkfish on deeper reefs could be an indication of mesopredator release, as the study's deep reef locations were within national reserves, which are open to some types of artisanal fishing, reducing the number of apex predators. There were specific ways each species was relating to their habitat and also we suggest that overfishing in deeper waters might be impacting their abundance positively. These species are not fished, but their predators are!

Kenya began to be the focus of my research and I spent significant time interacting with Benjo and the volunteers. Bobby and I had first visited Watamu in late 2010 and since that time I have been returning at least annually, sometimes twice a year. The family wanted to see the place and we also wanted to help the kids to experience other cultures. Thankfully, their school was on board, and we were able to take them to Kenya for about seven weeks in 2013/2014. We left cold and gray England on Boxing Day and arrived in a warm and sunny Watamu ready to explore and serve. The older children were very good swimmers and snorkelers, but Matthew was still very young. We decided that for this trip we would spend a lot of time in the rockpools on the edge of the beach in water close to shore. Little was known about these habitats, and we made a startling discovery that changed the course of A Rocha's work there for years to come.

Benjo had been looking for a coral species called the crisp pillow coral (*Anomastraea irregularis*) out on the reefs for a long time. It was endemic to the western Indian Ocean and Red Sea – meaning it was found nowhere else in the world. Our bias towards the nicer habitats meant that most of the volunteers wanted to do projects where they were snorkeling on the reefs or perhaps in seagrass habitats. However, at low tide, rock pools are revealed. These platforms of limestone become eroded, forming small pools, usually less than a meter squared which house interesting sea life. In many northern countries, this is the focus of much time and energy as the water is cold and often unclear offshore limiting exploration. But the team in Kenya had walked over these rockpools to get in the water and snorkel out to the reefs for years. On one fateful day, Benjo exclaimed that he had found the crisp pillow coral – it was hiding in plain sight, being walked near and around for years. It took having a small child in tow to get us to focus on this habitat.

We began to document the biodiversity of the rockpools and particularly focused on the crisp pillow coral – where was it found, how many, and what sizes. We were able to map the size and structure of the rockpools as part of our habitat mapping and then look at the distribution of these corals among them. I had learned much in England about faith and conservation and began to try and apply what I was learning to an integrated approach to the work in Kenya. While the species was of conservation value in terms of its ecological rarity, there didn't appear to be much value to humans. The coral was small, hidden, and not particularly beautiful. It didn't provide food and even the locals who tried to gain money from tourists by telling of the wonders of the rockpools never mentioned it. We began to develop a way of talking about our work as trying to make plain the "hidden things of God in the ocean." We saw that so much underwater is hidden from view and much of it had little or no value to humans. In Genesis God declares His creation good irrespective of its value to people. We wanted to focus on this small, non-descript species to highlight that we do not conserve wildlife or the environment because it helps us, but because of its value to God. If God loves and cares for His creation, so should we – whether it is beautiful or useful or not.

Walking down a typical beach, it would be easy to surmise that there is little living there. If it is a calm day, you might be looking out on the sea which resembles more a sheet of glass than an aquarium. Yet below your feet, crawling in and amongst the sand grains, swimming below the surface of the sea, and fixed to rocks just out of sight live an amazing array of marine creatures. All usually hidden from sight. For most of human history, the incredible biodiversity of the sea has remained hidden from sight or only seen on the end of a fisherman's line.

"There is the sea, vast and spacious, teeming with creatures beyond number – living things both large and small" (Psalm 104:25). It is easy to focus on the "large" aspect of this verse. Whales and dolphins or, for the more discerning, whale sharks and manta rays, fill us with awe at their size and power. Yet hidden from sight are innumerable "small" creatures that are equally amazing; their intrinsic value is not determined relative to us. They have value because they are God's creation (Psalm 104).

As we began studying the rockpools that are revealed at low tide, but remain hidden from sight at high tide, we found red algae, green algae, brown algae, sponges, coral, flatworms, crustaceans, marine worms, sea stars, brittle stars, sea cucumbers, sea urchins, sea squirts, and fish. Each is a major taxonomic group of marine organisms – all living in tiny rock pools hidden from sight. The hidden things of God in the ocean are revealed to those who search them out.

A Rocha Kenya had developed a great program to help alleviate pressure on local forests by providing scholarships for education to families that agreed not to harm them. These students would come to Mwamba for camps and often be taken out onto a boat for the first time to experience the coral reefs. This was expensive and often counterproductive as many were afraid to get in the water or had bad experiences with poor equipment. The rockpools provided a great way to do marine environmental education and were only a short walk away from the center. But we needed some resources.

Bobby and Sarah were still in elementary school but could use PowerPoint and other such programs. We gave them the project of developing a guide to the major taxonomic categories of species in the rockpools. So rather than a particular mollusk species, showing the various types of mollusks like clams or gastropods. They spent time exploring the rockpools and we took pictures to represent each group. They then put together a presentation that they gave to the center and which staff could use with young people visiting. They also put together a single-page back and front guide to these types of creatures that was laminated and used for education events. I think they are still used.

The rockpools also gave us an opportunity to try to put together a holistic project. I had shifted from a more dualistic and anthropocentric faith to faith in what some call the cosmic Christ. It is probably a bit of an unfortunate title that will put people off from investigating these ideas right from the start. But the "cosmic" part refers to Christ's rule throughout the universe and not just Lord over one species and planet. It also refers to the totality of the healing wrought from His death, resurrection, and ascension. All things that were broken at the fall were fixed at the cross, not just the relationship between one species in the universe and God. Holism then takes on a much bigger notion. Could we develop a project that involved healing the four relationships broken: with God, with other humans, with non-human creation, and with ourselves? Thus was born the Kenya Beach Boys project.

"Tourists aren't paying for trips, they are paying for information." Walking down the beach in Kenya, we were approached by Nemo, one of the Kenyan Beach Boys who participated in an introductory session on rockpool guiding. His statement is astounding as it represents a change in mindset after this training session. Many young men in the coastal region of Kenya leave school at an early age and try to make a living selling trips, curios, and sometimes themselves to tourists. Some are actually boys others older, but collectively they are referred to locally as Beach Boys. We want to help Nemo lift himself out of poverty by showing him and other Beach Boys the love of Christ through livelihood development, spiritual nurturing, and caring for the natural resources that his life depends upon.

Rockpools are accessible places where tourists can easily encounter marine life and consequently, an unofficial and informal local guiding industry has arisen, provided by "Beach

Boys". Kenyan Beach Boys come from a variety of cultural backgrounds representative of the area including Christian, Muslim, and Traditional religions, but are often marginalized in society and among the poorest economically. They can become involved in illicit activities that the tourism sector can cultivate, including drug dealing and prostitution. These young men rarely have access to resources or training that would enable them to develop sustainable jobs and thus remain in poverty.

Guiding for these Beach Boys is opportunistic work and offers a chance to sell snorkeling trips and terrestrial safaris to tourists. There are no defined charges or codes of conduct or any association. The Beach Boys have very limited knowledge about the environment where they are working. Given the conservation importance of the rockpools, their intrinsic worth, and their instrumental value to the local community, there is an opportunity here to show these young people "The hidden things of God in the ocean" so that this knowledge will benefit the place where they work and transform their lives.

We provided training sessions which were a mix of field-based training in the rockpools and classroom sessions covering species identification, ecology, resource use, business principles, and tourism issues. The beach boys were invited to participate in the life of the A Rocha community, stopping in for a cup of tea or even joining in with Bible studies if desired. To understand the damage to or changes to these habitats, a monitoring and research program for important species such as the crisp pillow coral was implemented.

This project had a number of successes, but ultimately failed as the Beach Boys were much more transient than we expected. Guiding tourists in the National Parks up north was much more lucrative and people left at the first chance. So, it was hard to develop a community. I think it was important, though, to try. We experiment, we learn, and then we can move ahead and make new mistakes. This process of learning is often as important as any so-called success.

I was committed, as was A Rocha Kenya, to finding Kenyan marine biologists to be a part of the project. One of the issues is that most of the university level education is based in the north of the country and many who are educated often don't spend much time in the water and thus are not prepared for ocean fieldwork. Add to that finding someone with a Christian commitment and it proved difficult over time to find the right person. However early on Peter Musembi joined the team and did great work going on to work with bigger international conservation NGOs. Eric Thuranira joined next, and he also excelled in bringing an organization and forward-thinking attitude to the work. He now works for a government agency in fisheries. Currently, Peter Musila has joined the team and he is excellent in the water obtaining grants and initiating a coral gardening project. It has been exciting to see that the norm now at A Rocha Kenya is for the main marine biologists to be Kenyan and any non-Kenyans involved assisting them in their work.

People seem to be fascinated by sharks. We received a few small grants over the years to study and protect these creatures and their relatives the rays. Of particular interest has been the Halavi guitarfish (*Glaucostegus halavi*) which is considered Critically Endangered on the IUCN Red List. This means that it is one step away from Extinct in the Wild. Why do we care about extinction? After all, throughout the spacetime of Earth many, many species have gone extinct. Yet Scripture seems to indicate that each of these species has a specific role to play ecologically (Psalm 104) and also spiritually as creatures who praise their maker, including within the new creation (Rev 5:9-14). So as followers of the Christ who these creatures praise and whose sacrifice on the cross would make all things right it does seem to most theologians that part of our service to God is to move the world towards how it will be. If there will be no extinction in the new creation, then we need to begin to move in that direction. It seems all the more clear when we consider that a creature like the Halavi guitarfish is Critically Endangered not because of natural selection, but because we have killed too many of them.

My daughter Sarah and I traveled to Kenya in 2016 for several weeks – again her teachers being very supportive – to do a survey of elasmobranchs (sharks and rays) in Watamu Marine National Park. We spent our days out on the research vessel Tewa, which is Swahili for grouper. This is a small motorboat that fits about 5 or 6 at most but is well suited for work in the shallows of the park. It was such fun as Sarah was now a young woman able to hold her own in the water and to engage with others as essentially an adult. Small observations can make a difference if you know what you are looking for. We saw very small rays in shallow water that indicated that there was spawning of that species nearby. Noting the juveniles of these species indicates that the Marine Park was serving as a nursery for small sharks and rays. We also saw many very small blacktip reef sharks and have subsequently been able to identify the rockpool areas in the south of the park as an important spawning and pupping ground for this species. Previous photos of very small Halavi guitarfish also made similar advances in our knowledge. You have to be out there and also understand what you are seeing. Time in the water is critical for really understanding these systems.

Kenya is where I really put together my spiritual life with my marine biology training. Much of what I did there was not scientifically new to me, but was important for setting the conservation agenda for the Watamu Marine National Park and A Rocha Kenya's marine conservation work. The time and specific location and camaraderie of other Christian scientists also allowed us to think wide and deep about how faith intersects with marine conservation. While in many ways England is my spiritual scientific home, these principles were applied specifically and refined practically in Kenya.

South of France

When you picture the south of France what comes to mind immediately? For me it is microplastics. This area of the world is renowned for its beautiful beaches and the blue of the Mediterranean Sea. All true, but look a bit closer, as we did, and you will find lots of microplastics. This was well-known to a few others, but for us was quite a shock.

A Rocha wanted to start a Mediterranean program linking up several national organizations and other potential countries in a project that could build across national borders. Dr Chris Walley was leading this adventure. I first came across Chris during my time in the UK, especially at St Madoc camp in Wales where he was a trustee. Chris is a geologist by training who emigrated to France with his wife Alison. They graciously hosted our family several times since then and were the main point of contact for a ten-day trip to see if there was a marine project that might be conducted as part of the potential Mediterranean program.

It was an arduous task – spend time along the coasts of France, Monaco, and Italy snorkeling and exploring to gather information about potential projects. I had gathered three young scientists to join whom I trusted both as friends and as experienced A Rocha marine team members. Benjamin Cowburn, Dorthea Seeger, and Aline Nussbaumer all volunteered significantly as part of the marine work in Kenya. They continue to this day to be involved in A Rocha marine work and the time in Kenya and the south of France significantly solidified those relationships. All three also slept on our floor multiple times in our small UK house, including a memorable few days when several others from the Marine Team joined us for a time of meetings – squeezing about 12 of us into a small UK house with one bathroom!

During this trip, we collected information on biodiversity, read literature on the threats to the Mediterranean Sea, made contacts with local groups and churches, and spent a lot of time in the water and eating good food. It wasn't lavish, but anyone who has been to that area of the world knows how good a baguette, cheese, and a few tomatoes can taste. We worked out of the, at the time, two French centers of Les Courmettes and Les Tourades. The latter has now been sold.

The Mediterranean is one of the most threatened seas with a long history of people interacting with its water and creatures therein. Significantly, for Christians, a decent chunk of the New Testament happens in and around the Mediterranean. We don't think of Israel as having a seaside coast and none of the four synoptic gospels feature any narrative on the coast, but Paul's trips certainly do. It can be hard sitting on a beautiful beach looking out over the beautiful blue water to understand that overfishing is decimating the fish populations, that runoff from land bringing chemicals and nutrients into the sea is changing habitats, and that warming water is causing some of the more northern species to move closer towards extinction. Yet there is still so much beauty under the water. In 2022 the International Forum for A Rocha was held at Les Courmettes and it was such a privilege to go with a small group down to the sea on our day off and show them that beauty – some experiencing snorkeling for the first time ever. The exclamations of joy and surprise were priceless. These hidden threats and beauty make it harder, though, to convince people that something is wrong. If the same level of change were to happen on land it would be so much more noticeable – we still may not do anything about it, but that is another issue.

We settled on two potential projects involving on the one hand studying the bivalve *Pinna nobilis*, the largest clam in Europe reaching sizes up to 1 meter, and microplastics. It is hard to imagine now, but in my training at the University of Miami and even during my ten years in South Asia the issue of plastic pollution was not a thing. We can look back now at some pioneers who saw the growing problem, but for the most part, the marine science community was not focused on this issue as they are today and to be fair, the problem was not as large as it is today. So, while we swam in the beautiful Mediterranean and saw the huge threats from overfishing, other types of pollution, and climate change, we realized that we could develop a low-cost project immediately and begin contributing to reducing plastic pollution. A Rocha has typically focused on species and habitats and so there was some resistance to a project focusing on a threat. I also did not properly link the microplastic work to species and habitat conservation – a beach cleanup really is habitat restoration. Some better marketing on my part might have helped internally. But there was enough support and having made the trip in September of 2015, amazingly by November of that year we had two volunteers in place at Les Courmettes moving forward on a microplastics project. Aline Nussbaumer is English by nationality, but grew up in France and volunteered to lead the project. We were contacted by a university student Samantha Mellender who had a six-month paid internship they could use anywhere and wanted to use it to help A Rocha. She was willing to head to Les Courmettes as well and was a great boost to the project.

It has always been a joy and privilege of my work that at times I can take members of my family with me on trips. My daughter Heather and I returned to Les Courmettes to continue to work with Aline and Samantha some months later looking to choose some sites in Italy that we might work in along with continuing to explore the short Monaco coast and the small part of France between it and Italy. I didn't realize the Mediterranean ever got cold, but in December of 2016, we experienced why the beaches are not crowded at all. Heather wrote a number of adventure blogs for A Rocha as a young explorer, and we enjoyed snorkeling in seagrass beds looking particularly for shallow water sites to study *Pinna nobilis*. I still have not given up on studying that species, but we have yet to develop a proper study. One day in Italy we met a fisher coming out of the water with octopuses hanging off his weight belt. He had been spearfishing and collecting them. Aline had a long conversation with him, and we were able to see firsthand the two sides of the coin that is artisanal fishing. Here was a person, trying to feed their family by going out and gathering a small number of lucrative species to sell or eat. But we knew how when you multiply that times hundreds or thousands of people over large areas the impact can still be significant. How do we balance the needs of families and support this smaller level of take while continuing to battle against the larger factory vessels that commercially take thousands of times more in the same amount of time? Yet other families who do not or cannot go out into the water to gather their own food also want to eat seafood which is provided by these factory vessels.

We based the fieldwork portion for the microplastics work out of Les Tourades, A Rocha's center near a region known as the Camargue. You wouldn't think that there were flamingos in France – but there they were. This is a beautiful area of National Park with wetlands and stunning beaches. It is also very close to the Rhone River which is a major source of microplastic input into the Mediterranean. This meant spending some time in very industrial areas at the river mouth where there were loads of microplastics. We began to use nurdle hunts to quickly index microplastic pollution. By this time Samantha's internship was over and Dr Joanna Calcutt had joined the team. Jo was a biologist with more of a lab background and she had spent the previous several years in Indonesia working to develop sea cucumber mariculture. Jo brought a desire and love of the microscope which neither Aline nor I had, and she enjoyed processing our samples. I remained mostly in the UK just making a few trips down taking the Eurostar to Paris from London and then taking the train to the coast – it was as fantastic as it sounds. The fast train from Paris to the coast can reach speeds of 200 mph and sitting with a baguette and a bottle of wine watching the countryside pass was pleasurable indeed.

The methodology developed was to lay two 100-meter transects along the high tide strand line on sandy beaches of The

Camargue area. Along each transect, five randomly selected 50 centimeter by 50 centimeter quadrats were dug to a depth of 5 centimeters, and all sand was sieved through both a 5 millimeter and 1 millimeter geological grade sieve in order to collect the fraction of sediment and attendant microplastics within that size range. Metal and other non-plastic equipment were used to avoid contamination. Seawater was first filtered through a 300-micron filter in order to avoid contamination from the ocean. The resultant material was taken back to our field study center and clean water made to a seawater salinity was used to float the microplastics. These were then collected and examined under a stereomicroscope and classified into categories.

While this methodology was useful for the accurate categorization of microplastics to a level that could be published in peer-reviewed literature, other types of activities would be necessary for engaging the average person in citizen science-based activities. It should be said, that even though the much more precise methodology just presented was less amenable to a non-scientist, those without scientific training were often involved in the research and the activity itself generated enough interest from beachgoers that we had to designate someone to be the "educator" for the day answering the many questions so that others could continue to work unimpeded. The primary non-technical, citizen science method we began to use was that developed by FIDRA for their Great Nurdle Hunt. This involves searching for nurdles, plastic pellets used as the basis for all plastic products, on the beach, recording length of time, location, number of participants, and number of nurdles found. This method is simple and while searching for one type of microplastic, sensitizes the observer to the multitude of other types of microplastics and general plastic pollution on the beach.

Alongside these scientific enterprises, we developed several theological resources to engage Christians with a value-based understanding of how Christian principles apply to the global plastic pollution problem. This involved taking passages from the Bible and developing a question-based format for engaging people in a thoughtful exercise of applying principles to a specific issue. Additionally, several prayers were written that address very specific problems of plastic pollution in the ocean, and which could be used before, during, or after research and conservation activities.

We wanted to share this experience with others and Aline developed a retreat on plastics that she was only able to run one time unfortunately, gathering several people from across Europe to spend the week at Les Tourades learning about plastic pollution, studying what the Bible says about it (surprisingly a lot), and collecting data using multiple methods that could be used by participants upon their return to their home countries. This type of immersive experience is so important for helping people to really get it and to pass on practical knowledge. Aline and Jo sought funding for the project, but it was difficult to find enough and eventually, we began to realize that the project needed to end. Both Aline and Jo were volunteering time and not paid over several years with A Rocha France helping significantly through some paid jobs and reduced costs at the center for food and lodging. We knew we had an important set of ideas and procedures that others in A Rocha could use and my experience in knowledge management made me loathe to lose all that tacit knowledge – the experience and information inside Aline and Jo's brains. We needed to make some of it explicit and did so by taking the most important ideas and building a Microplastics Toolbox, which is now in its second version as a Plastics Toolbox. Aline and Jo made one trip to Portugal to train the team there in the techniques after Cindy and I had visited A Rocha's center Cruzinha and found a desire to work on microplastics.

Ultimately, I would continue to use this same protocol and Toolbox in Florida and Michelle Feenstra who is the daughter of longtime friends was trained and spent six months in Kenya conducting the first microplastics survey on that coast. Many have used the Toolbox to learn about plastic pollution and its spiritual significance.

There is a really nice coffee shop near the entrance to Lambeth Palace on the south side of the River Thames in London. We had visited many times, passing by the large doors signaling the entrance to the home and office of the Archbishop of Canterbury, the highest-ranking clergy in the Church of England. This time, though, I was actually invited to enter those doors – along with a number of others who were convened by the archbishop to talk about plastic pollution. There was a growing awareness of plastic pollution and its impact, particularly in Europe. This culminated in the UK as part of the Blue Planet effect – a noticeable rise in awareness and changes of habit related to plastic pollution after the BBC documentary showed an episode focused on the topic. The day was an interesting mix of talks from the front and at tables with the main intent being to gather scientists, clergy, and policymakers in the same room and see what comes of it. Not all were from the church, which made for a great mix. The highlight for me was meeting Rev. Dr. Winston Halapua, the former archbishop of Polynesia and author of an amazing book called *Waves of God's Embrace*.

Several groups gathered afterward, with A Rocha and Tearfund and a few others looking to stimulate Christian thought and action on the topic. Much of the work by groups other than A Rocha has continued to focus on the impact on humans – and it is significant. Hundreds of thousands of needless deaths are linked to plastic pollution via many unexpected avenues. For example, plastic pollution blocks sewers in developing countries resulting in standing water and an increase in mosquito-borne illness and death. Yet it remains true that God cares for all His creatures. Every species that has been examined for evidence of plastic impact has been found. Exploration of every habitat, from the top of Everest to the bottom of the Marianas Trench has found impact. We are thorough!

I tried to pull together what I had learned about plastic

pollution in a small booklet published by Grove Books and uncreatively called *Marine Plastics*. My focus was to look at how plastic pollution impacts the four relationships that are broken and need healing: with God, each other, non-human creation, and ourselves. Plastic impacts all of these relationships for good and for ill. What is the role of both science and faith in this healing? You will have to read the whole booklet to get the details, but part of what I wrote describing the structure of the booklet indicates my hope for those who do read it.

"While we will spend some time thinking about the ways in which plastic is negatively impacting these relationships – science often pointing this out – our focus will be on a positive vision of what we are working towards and indicating the potential role plastic might play in their restoration. Plastic will not go away, both literally as we see in the overview on plastic above, but also in terms of our use as a society. We have created plastic and it is now a part of our lives and ecosystems. We will thus focus on exploring how to use plastic in a way that becomes part of the healing of these relationships, or at least is not part of their destruction.

The first relationship we will examine is with nature. We will look at this particularly from an ecological view and examine selected writings of Michael Northcott and Richard Bauckham as they describe theologically how we should relate to animals as we ourselves, of course, are an animal too and part of the community of creation. We then turn our attention to our neighbor and engage with Pope Francis's vision of Our Common Home – also known as Laudato Si. How can plastic enhance our relationships with other humans rather than hurt them, particularly in caring for the poor and marginalized? Wisdom literature has, well, much wisdom! We examine portions of the Job and Proverbs to discover plastic's impact on our relationship with God and within ourselves.

These relationships that were broken at the fall are healed through the cross. The Conclusion brings these reflections together in discussion, pointing out some of the ways forward to use plastic for good in the healing of these four relationships particularly focusing on Ecochurches. The call is to move from environmentalism in general and "obsession" with plastic pollution in particular as a niche within the church towards integration into all Christian endeavors as part of Glorifying God and serving him. A Rocha's Plastic Toolbox will serve as a practical toolkit for anyone wishing to pursue this course of action. A short epilogue looks at the role of plastic in crises – both the current one (COVID-19), but also more generally as this will certainly not be the last and Christians regularly engage in relief efforts after events such as earthquakes, storms, and famine.

My own experience is as a marine biologist and much of my role in the past number of years has been to study and develop projects to combat plastic pollution in the ocean. Much of what will follow is with an ocean focus – it does, after all, occupy 71% of the surface of our planet! The principles and theological reflection I believe transcend habitats. You will see that the problem of plastic in the ocean is a problem of plastic on the land. My hope is that you will be inspired to continue to live in a way that your use of plastic glorifies God, is restorative of your relationships, and leads to a life of fullness in Christ."

Portugal

Who knew that a small house in a relatively remote and to me unknown part of Europe would feature so significantly in my life. I am currently re-reading Under the Bright Wings by Peter Harris which details the first nine years of A Rocha in Portugal. As Peter, Miranda, and many others joined to begin the field study center called Cruzinha, I was going along my merry way in high school and off to university and a life in South Asia not even becoming aware of this work until almost 25 years into it.

Cindy and I traveled to Portugal in early 2017. The microplastics project was continuing to progress. We wondered if the team there in Portugal would be interested in starting a similar project monitoring the beaches near the Alvor Estuary. I had brought some equipment with me to show the methodology and to leave behind so they could begin. There were a number of European Service Volunteers and this seemed a good project and has consistently been able to win funding for these volunteers to come and do the work. I was eager for Cindy to experience Cruzinha and we enjoyed good times of food, fun, and fellowship with Marcial and Paula.

My second visit to Portugal came during the 2018 Leaders Forum which was being held near Lisbon. Still holding on to one aspect of my Americanness, I rented a car after and along with a few others, including Marcial Felguires who leads A Rocha Portugal, drove down to Cruizinha. We stopped along the way for a traditional Portuguese meal and enjoyed seeing the cork tree forests and the beautiful, if dry, interior of that country. In many ways, the field study center is underwhelming. The property is not huge, the buildings not grand, and much in a state of disarray. Yet two rooms of note change everything as you experience the hospitality around the grand table that Miranda bought so long ago and which she, posthumously, and her daughter and my current colleague Jo

Swinney write about in *A Place at the Table*. The second room is the library which has many comfy couches and a fireplace that brings warmth to the room during the surprisingly cool winter months.

My oldest son Bobby was meeting me in Portugal, and I went to pick him up at the Faro airport. His trip was more frantic than necessary as he found out on the bus to the airport in the UK that he had forgotten his passport! Thankfully friends drove it out to him and he made his flight. The Algarve, as the southern Portuguese coast is known, is famous for cliff jumping. We had done our research and found a few places that weren't exceedingly high. I dislike heights intensely and so like a good child, Bobby made sure to stress me out with his climbing and jumping. I joined at a couple places, taking ten times the length of time to make it to the jumping-off point and then virtually being pushed off by Bobby so that I would actually jump. Once you are in the air it is fine as there is no choice at that point.

Portugal has become one of my favorite places in the world. The beaches are studded with eroded rocks that change colors with the movement of the sun. The ocean is surprisingly cold until you look at a map and realize that Portugal is not, in fact, on the Mediterranean Sea and that it faces the North Atlantic with currents running down the coast from the cold north. The Algarve is sheltered from big Atlantic waves which Portugal's east coast receives, including the biggest of them all at Nazare'. Another colleague Julio Reis lives nearby that place and I was able to visit, though not in the 100-foot wave season.

The center is located on an estuary that has sandy beaches and dunes separating it from the Atlantic. One of the major issues impacting coastal and marine habitats globally is land use changes, particularly for development. This is especially the case in the Algarve. Peter Harris says that you can see A Rocha's work from space. By that, he means that if you use satellite maps to look at the Algarve you see development after development after development – except in one place near Cruzinha. A Rocha has collected data and led court battles to protect this area from development based on its value intrinsically and instrumentally. Without the science to back up claims of the importance to the area, it would now look like the nearby towns built to the hilt and lacking in wildlife.

The idea of Cruzinha looms large in a relatively small number of people compared to the global population, but within certain circles, it has a mystique and most come back from trips there not disappointed. While trying to run a center like Cruzinha can be exhausting and over the long term quite difficult, the impact on those you are serving is significant. This doesn't mean it is always "worth it" and for many life at a center is for a season. We have tried to implement that sort of hospitality with our home and have enjoyed a huge number of people staying with us in Florida where we now live. We have a wall with handprints on it of most of the people who have stayed with us over the years. We began after Peter and Miranda stayed with us, so right now there is a beautiful butterfly painting in one corner in memory of Miranda and a spot next to it waiting for Peter to visit again and place his handprint there. Jo Swinney and her late mother Miranda write in their book *A Place at the Table* about the centrality of hospitality in the Christian life particularly in the story of A Rocha.

Our daughter Heather was able to experience and give that hospitality during a three-month stay at Cruzinha during her gap year. She worked with a Dutch student to study plastic pollution. I wrangled a work trip during her time there and we spent a week visiting beaches along the whole Algarve coast conducting nurdle hunts and microplastic research. You can go to the Great Nurdler website and see our observations among the many thousands globally. At this time, we are the only ones to have done nurdle hunts in that area of the world. We enjoyed simple meals together during the day – usually bread, cheese, and some sort of dried meat. Time with my kids doing conservation and exploring beautiful places is such a privilege.

Not as intensely, but somewhat similarly, our kids have always been a part of the work we have done. In India, they went along on all our visits to Maldivian households. In England, they slept on the floor so visitors could stay in their beds and often walked up into the hills to help with juniper planting or other conservation work. They have nurdled all over the world and family beach days used to start with a nurdle hunt. Here in Florida, they also live in community with visitors and our interns. They say they love it and wouldn't have it any other way. The same with my travel. For much of their life, I was away $1/6^{th}$ of the time or about 2 months a year, though not in a row! I don't think they are just telling me what I want to hear – they are proud of the work and what we are accomplishing and want me to be happy too. Cindy has always been supportive, but obviously, the brunt of the difficulties with that amount of travel fell to her. In India, we were often together for the travel, but with the kids joining school in England, someone needed to be there. I am grateful for that sacrifice and service.

Sea of Cortez, Mexico

Our quarry lay ahead, a long, thin shape near the surface of the water its distinctive white spotted pattern showing clearly. This was a smaller individual, some 7 meters (20 feet) in length, about half the size of the maximum. We had been driving up and down a particular coastline searching for an hour or so and finally had found a whale shark. Our guide, known for his care for these species and concern not to cause harm due to boat collisions or too close human contact instructed us to get in the water with our snorkel gear and follow him.

These sharks are the largest of all fish and have huge mouths – with very tiny teeth. Their prey is the tiny planktonic animals causing the murkiness in the water. These whale sharks find patches of dense food and spend time swimming through them sucking in huge amounts of water and filtering out the tiny animals for their meal. The pace is usually leisurely from a fish's perspective, yet still a brisk swimming pace for a human. We swam with this individual and others who joined us for a long time. If I had a bucket list, this would have been on that list – yet I confess to still feeling like the experience was manufactured.

How do tourism, wildlife experiences, and adventure go together? I had a similar feeling visiting a game park in South Africa. Yes, it is true these animals were in a massively large area, living in habitats they would normally live in, feeding off each other and the land – but there was a fence. These whale sharks were not fenced in, yet the tour guides knew about the place where they were often found and we went there especially to see this. In a slightly more manufactured way, my experience in Hawaii swimming with manta rays at night felt similar. These huge animals had been attracted by the lights of nearby hotels which congregated plankton and so chose to be there – but the boat with its line of buoys to hold on to and additional lights to bring the animals even closer seems more like an experience you might find somewhere like Seaworld. Maybe I value serendipity in animal encounters. Does the manta ray that just happened to swim by me in the Maldives while doing my research count as a more authentic experience? It feels that way and yet there are endemic species (only found in that place) that you would only see if you specifically went there to see them. The Bangui cardinalfish springs to mind only found around a few isolated islands in Indonesia – and now through the aquarium industry in most pet shops in the world. Does going down to my local pet shop and seeing the Bangui Cardinalfish count as actually having seen it?

The whale sharks in question were near La Paz Mexico in Baja California. I had traveled there not just to see these species, but primarily to learn from and see if I could partner with Steve Dresselhaus, a long-time resident of the area and one of the few others in the world with marine missions experience. Steve had started a Mexican NGO that was using ocean adventures to bring about transformed lives and communities. The hope was that A Rocha could partner with the NGO to engage local university students more scientifically and integrate better marine conservation into their projects and programs. Steve is an avid kayaker and diver so a fun-filled, exhausting, two weeks was spent trying to keep up with him. He introduced me to what he calls Gorilla Diving. We haul the kayaks and SCUBA gear out to a particular beach and load up the kayaks with our kit. The idea is then to paddle out to the diving area, kit up in the water, make a dive, and then get the gear back in the kayak and paddle back to shore. It is a lot of work, but a great experience made more special by the beauty of the surroundings, the company, and the unique flora and fauna of Baja California.

Time with Steve was both refreshing and exhausting. He has clearly found joy in the absolute focus on one place and even on just a few activities. Like many successful ventures, many people outside of it want to try and grow it or expand it. Thankfully he is resisting that and reveling in his place. It can be hard to say no to opportunities and lose focus when things get going well. I often struggle to stay the course. We do need to know when it is time to cut our losses. That is one of the huge lessons that my Professor at Miami taught me. She would often talk about needing to cut her losses and just move on. My recent Professor of sorts, Seth Godin, talks about it as sunk costs. This is obviously not original to him, but he speaks of it in terms of a life of creativity. His definition of sunk costs is a gift from your former self. You spend a lot of energy and time on something and so it feels like you should just keep going with it. But you often do that at the cost of other better opportunities. Just look at that energy and time as a gift and move on.

Our kayaking work in Florida is inspired by the work in Baja. When we moved to Titusville I knew that I was giving up on easy diving research. There would be some hard-core diving nearby, but it would be really difficult, expensive, and probably not as much fun as working a few hours south of us. However, there is water everywhere and lots of beauty in and around it that can be experienced by kayak. While Steve has focused on the adventure aspect of the kayaking our work here is more related to the Bluemind or Blue Spaces/Blue Health concepts. There is a huge amount of research that nature and natural spaces are good for mental, emotional, physical, and spiritual health. It turns out that at least in some studies, blue spaces have a greater impact on these than green spaces. Certainly, get out for a walk in the forest, but if you can walk by the ocean or ideally go for a swim, all the better. It isn't just ocean water, though. Taking a bath, being by a fountain, or even near or in a swimming pool. Just get on, in, near, or under the water. Our desire was to help people begin to heal their relationships with God, each other, nature, and themselves through time on, in, near, or under the water. When visitors come, we will head out kayaking or to the beach. One of my colleagues Brittany Michalski lived with us for a significant time and she has developed an experience of kayaking that incorporates scientific and theological reflection, focusing on interacting with knowledge about what they are seeing interspersed with times of silence and the reading of Psalm 104. We also try to make sure if we are working on the beach that we factor in some time to jump in, swim, and just have a lie down in quiet on the beach. Incorporating these rhythms into the work and life in Florida has helped me through many stressful times. An additional practice we have with the interns is to start some "meetings" with our feet in our swimming pool. Starting in silence, experiencing the water, and then talking about what we need to talk about.

I really wanted to take Matthew to Madagascar. But then COVID hit and it became difficult – so Baja served as a substitute. We spent the night in transit at the Dallas airport sleeping as we could and then arrived in Cabo San Lucas. We were going to spend the first part of the trip with Matthew surfing and then the last part with Steve Dresselhaus in La Paz. We got on several wrong buses before we found our way to the downtown. I had decided that we would do this trip all by public transport. We eventually found our way to the main bus station and took the bus about an hour and a half north along the west coast where I had reserved a room at a surf camp and where the surfing was supposed to be good that time of year. Well, of course, it was not and it was best back in Cabo. We ended up starting and ending each day with a long bus ride to and from Cabo but found a great spot for him to surf.

Matthew thoroughly enjoyed the surfing, even the unplanned exit through the rocky area full of sea urchins which ended with one of the surf store workers spending an hour pulling spines out of his feet. The public transport was relatively easy once we figured it out, even if it meant lots of our time. We often had tacos in the evening and enjoyed the tired sleep that water and travel bring. We then bused over to La Paz and Steve Dresselhaus met us at the station. Some of the animal experiences I had hoped to share with Matthew didn't materialize – being somewhat hypocritical in my desire to take Matt to a specific place to see specific animals, given the discussion above. The whale sharks had moved on during covid and the dive spot with sea lions was closed so that a film crew could use it. The trip previous, we had a memorable time diving around a rocky area that housed a colony of sea lions. At various times one of these sleek, fast, and curious animals would pop down in front of you and check out what you were doing. It was another amazing animal experience that I had hoped Matthew could enjoy. We did do several scuba dives together and one long kayak trip with some snorkeling over beautiful coral reefs. Our departure was almost doomed by a hurricane, but we got some of the last planes out before they closed the airport for a few days.

I will probably return to Baja in the future, but the focus might be more on Cabo Pulmo. On my original trip, Steve and I dove there in a marine protected area that serves as a classic example of protection from fishing. This small fishing village at the tip of the peninsula had decimated the marine environment and continued to live in poverty and hunger. Researchers and conservationists began to work with them to talk about the potential benefits of protecting the reefs both for eventual fishing surrounding the reserve and to increase their livelihoods through ecotourism. The life in the reserve has come back and fishing surrounding the reserve has become sustainable.

We don't usually think of our societies as stratified, but they often are economically. There are clearly those with tons of money that can easily know about and take advantage of new economic opportunities. It often takes money to make money. But there is what at least used to be called a "creamy layer" in development circles. Not all poor are equally poor. If you were to go as a foreigner into a village to look at development and wanted to focus on "the poor" (also a contentious term) you might end up partnering with someone or some group to move ahead. From all economic and social indicators, they are poor, yet within that society, they are the "creamy layer" of the poor that rises to the surface. Maybe they know a little more English or have some distant relative in the government who can help with permits or other resources that separate them from the rest of "the poor."

Who benefits from declaring a marine reserve? Who has the resources to make enough changes to their fishing boat that tourists might be attracted or knows enough English that Gringos are comfortable heading out to sea with them? Development is fraught with these potential issues where we end up not doing what we really intended. I do not know if this is the case in Cabo Pulmo as I haven't spent significant time there or studied the nuances. However, it is something we have had to think about a lot as we work in places where outside money can flow into situations where tens or hundreds of dollars can make massive differences in long-term survival. I am grateful for my time in Baja and the inspiration that the place and its people were for our future work in Florida.

Titusville Florida USA

We currently live in Titusville Florida. For most of my life, I didn't know it existed. The southern end of the south, this smallish city east of Orlando and across the Indian River Lagoon from Kennedy Space Center had eluded me. We decided we were going to move from living in England and considered many options globally but thought we would give being back in the USA a try. I wanted to be nearer warm water to do research more often and it would be nice to be back near family again. With a limited budget and realizing we did not want to live in South Florida again, we looked more centrally and focused on the Atlantic coast as it had significant waves whereas the west coast of Florida is more pacific and in places we could afford, mostly lined with mangrove forests. Titusville was still recovering from the collapse of the Space Shuttle program and so prices were lower than in most places. From a scientific standpoint, I knew it would mean less diving as the coral reefs of Florida stop about 2 or 3 hours south of this point. But it seemed there were enough interesting habitats and species to move forward – it has turned out to be very interesting indeed.

While at the University of Miami, I made one trip with the SCUBA club up to Crystal River to dive with manatees and had over the years visited some springs near where Cindy grew up north of Tampa. There was also a memorable dive trip during university where I went to stay with a close friend Shadd Whitehead in the Florida panhandle. We dove Vortex springs. I don't think I would do it now, but you go into a main cavern and then there is a long tunnel extending deep within the earth. Much of the dangerous side passages are blocked off and there is a line cemented into the bottom, but it is completely dark so you need lights and do not want to stir up the muck on the bottom or suffer a complete blackout even with the lights. At our turnaround time, we were at over a 100-foot depth and fairly far back into the cavern. We "surfaced" in an air pocket that was caused by divers exhaling over so many years and had a good laugh together. Our return to Florida saw exploration of the springs on a new breadth and consistent companionship by that loved marine mammal, the manatee.

There are four species of manatee in the Atlantic, three of them on Africa's west coast and one related species, the dugong, which occurs from East Africa to the western Pacific. These animals are mentioned in the Bible, the early Tabernacle used sea cow hides as tent material and these must have come from dugongs in the Red Sea as there are none in the Mediterranean, or perhaps from traders from the Middle East. There was a species living on the Alaska coast hundreds of years ago, called the Stellar Sea Cow. This animal grew up to 10 meters in length and could, reportedly, feed an entire ship for a month. They were reported by European fishing fleets first in 1741 and went extinct in the next 27 years. One more voice in the orchestra of praise gone out. The manatee in Florida seemed to be going in that direction. There was a great number of manatees in the past extending throughout the Caribbean and West Indies. Hence the formal common name is West Indian Manatee. Some think because of this name that they were never native to Florida and thus an "invader" causing a strong pushback by some groups about manatee love. But this is absolutely false.

We have enjoyed kayaking with manatees, watching them from the shore, and swimming with them. One memorable occasion for the rest of the Sluka family was in one of our usual Florida Springs swimming holes – Blue Springs State Park. In the winter you cannot swim in the crystal-clear spring, since there are hundreds of manatees there and they rather suspect that many *Homo sapiens* would not be able to restrain themselves and cause too much distress to these creatures – a good assumption. You can swim in the spring other times, though, and sometimes manatees will swim up to the spring head. You are supposed to not approach the animals – and would be given a big fine if you did harass it – but if they come to you… Well, everyone but me got a snuggle from this one manatee that clearly wanted to play.

Cindy was near the dock and the manatee came right up to her wrapped its flippers around her legs and gave them a nice snuggle, whiskers playfully scratching at her legs. I was the only one that missed out! We sometimes would camp at Blue Springs, and you could go down to the spring before the hoards arrived and one day I had the whole area to myself – except my manatee companion. This was a rescue manatee indicated by the GPS tag tied to its tail reporting its position to researchers sitting behind a computer in some lab somewhere. I spent a long time just hanging out with this creature and she clearly wanted to snuggle, though I was good and did not reach out and touch her. At one point we were eye to eye and she was definitely going in for a big kiss. Was a great moment, even for a proper marine biologist – we all know that real marine biologists don't have feelings for marine mammals, we are too cool for that, especially "smiling" dolphins.

The manatee is also a great example that conservation works. The number of manatees statewide continued to drop and if you have ever seen a manatee, you know that they have long and deep scars across their back from boats hitting them. Floridians seem to think that they have a right to fish and boat anywhere taking as much and going as fast as they please. Well, imagine speeding along a canal and then running into a huge manatee. It isn't hard to work out who comes out the worst. Researchers documented that the main death cause for manatees was indeed boat collisions. A series of manatee slow-down zones was developed and low and behold, manatee deaths decreased. Another example of science helping us to love God and love our neighbor.

Last night we took some family out kayaking in the bioluminescence. During the ten years we lived in Miami, I had never heard that you could do this near Titusville. It is a secret of central Florida, it seems. It takes a decent amount of preparation to bring a group out kayaking at night, especially as the best nights to see the glowing water are the darkest. The kayaks need to be loaded on a trailer and secured, glow sticks prepared and safety equipment checked. Ironically, the best bioluminescence seems to be right at the kayak launch site! The oohs and aahs on seeing the glowing water are always worth the trip. A decent wind was blowing last night which made kayaking a bit more challenging, but it rewarded with the waves glowing and ridges of light with each crest making the lagoon shine. Fish could be seen swimming away from the kayaks and when startled in shallow water. We went to our usual spot for the best lights and there was nothing – except heavy breathing. I doubt they were correlated, but the calm dark area which usually shines brightest had no bioluminescence – but it did seem to have a group of manatees sleeping. They are not dangerous, of course, except if you kayak over them in shallow water and wake them up and they decide to flee in panic. We turned and went back to other areas. This night was relatively cloudy with only a few glimpses of stars, but we have been out on other nights where the night sky was as spectacular as the water.

Daytime kayaking has its delights too. It is rare that one doesn't see several dolphins hunting and the manatees are always a treat. We are in the midst of exploring the beneficial impacts of water on our mental, physical, spiritual, and emotional health. It makes sense that if 71% of the planet is water and much of animal bodies as well, and if we have a good God at least as we define that, then it would be the case that being in, on, near, or under the water would bring wellbeing. The idea of nature impacting our wellbeing is not new and has been well studied in "green" spaces, but like most ideas, much less explored in "blue" spaces. As we seek to help people thrive in their relationships with God, each other, nature, and themselves, how can water play a role in that healing? Keep an eye out for more on this in the future or be a part of the experiments. We try to integrate this idea into all we are doing.

Who knew that Titusville was the center of horseshoe crab abundance and spawning for the state of Florida? I sure didn't. We arrived in Titusville in 2017 just before Christmas and I began to volunteer with a project called Linked with Limulus or Horseshoe Crab Watch – Limulus being part of the scientific name of this species. These are not actually crabs, but more closely related to spiders and scorpions. They aren't dangerous and have no fangs or venom. They scuttle their way along the bottom mostly unchanged for millions of years eating what they can, making more horseshoe crabs, and trying not to be eaten. Much of the Indian River Lagoon's periphery has been heavily modified to prevent erosion and so there are very few areas of sand where these creatures can come ashore and lay their eggs. Turns out Titusville bridge is just such a place and on a good evening, when the wind is blowing the right direction at the right speed thousands come ashore, digging into the sand and depositing eggs and sperm that will grow into the next generation. We assist those tasked with monitoring the statewide population and get a chance to tag individuals to see if we can determine where they are moving. I set a task for our interns to spend some time not studying them, but to sit among them and listen and watch. A very moving poem came out of this time by one of our interns Alli Cutting and was made into a great video by another Michaela Stenerson. I think this is also where Bluemind well-being and creatureliness can come together – taking time to sit, listen, learn, and reflect. That reflection often needs to be intentional, especially if it is integrated into spirituality. Some may immediately feel or understand those bonds between creatures and the Creator through these experiences, but I sense it is something we have lost over time and certainly isn't often taught in churches. I spent a great deal of time learning how to study God's Book of Words, but essentially none within a church context about how to study His Book of Works, despite the repeated remonstrations from the Book of Words to do so.

You will notice a distinct hole in our data collection centered around entrance 13 to Playalinda Beach. No, not superstitious, just trying to avoid naked people. Driving into our local beach, which also happens to be part of Canaveral National Seashore part of the National Park System, you see a sign warning that you might see nudity at the end of the road. Cindy went for a run and realized her location a bit too late. I am not opposed to nudity at all but might be hard to ask interns and staff to strip off so we could contextualize our data collecting. Nudity notwithstanding, the beaches of Playalinda are spectacular scenery with typical sandy beach characteristics of a sand dune covered in salt-resistant vegetation flowing into sand lined with a high tide strand line of seaweed washed up at the last tide and flowing into the beautiful water. It is, though, a low biodiversity beach as is most of the Atlantic coast of Florida. Imagine trying to live in an environment that is smashed by waves, water moving in with the tides and then out exposing you to the sun, and sand grains moving all the time. Biodiversity on sandy beaches is determined most by three physical facts: the type of sand, orientation to the waves, and slope of the beach. Imagine a calm beach protected from strong wave action, with very fine-grained sediment which can catch and keep organic material (ie. food), and a rich, large area exposed at each tide – you would have lots of life. Playalinda is the opposite as it is directly exposed to any major storm system as evidenced by the hurricanes of 2022 which wiped out a large portion of the sand dunes and beach access infrastructure due to huge waves. The sand grains are large which means that small creatures can't live amongst these boulders in proportion to their size. This impacts the food chain and the amount of organic matter that can feed small creatures. You therefore have in the sand a few species of crabs, some worms at low tide, and several molluscs, particularly coquina shells which form some of the distinctive coquina rock used to decorate many Florida gardens.

While it isn't a particularly great place for biodiversity, it does a good job of collecting plastic! The Orlando crowd on the weekends leaves some of it, but most wash up on the beach after a storm. This plastic is just as likely to come from the Caribbean or even Europe as the North Atlantic gyre, a circulating mass of water in the North Atlantic, collects everything that comes out of rivers surrounding it and transports it to other places. A roulette wheel of destruction – where will it land? This is about loving your neighbors. You have the neighbors in the ocean who on one hand can benefit from the new attachment surface, but on the other choke and die on it. Many small marine species need some place to stick to and if they don't find it die if not eaten beforehand. So, you will find large pieces of plastic that wash up with goose barnacles or other creatures living on and in the plastic. But you also find that baby sea turtles wash back up on our beaches with stomachs full of plastic they have eaten dying prematurely and due to our negligence. I may pick up plastic on my local beach that someone in Portugal might toss away thoughtlessly or more likely the wind takes away from a beach picnic unnoticed. Most people think of the oceans as separating us, but I have learned from reading Pacific Island literature, particularly an amazing book by Winston Halapua called *Waves of God's Embrace*, that the oceans connect us. The water currents move from one place to another allowing travel in the past by canoe or sail – this also means plastic can follow the same trails. So much can, and has been said by me, about plastic pollution in another chapter, I will simply say we do need to turn off the plastic tap, but the best solution right now to the plastic that is already in the ocean is to wait for it to wash up, pick it up, and get it into a landfill that will make sure it doesn't go anywhere else. It isn't a great solution, but it is the best one we have right now.

One of the delights of the past several years in Titusville has been collaborating with others who share a passion for this area. The horseshoe crab project was the first I was involved in and during the 2018 spawning season it was mainly three of us that collected the data. This was an established project run by the IFAS/UF and FWC. Myself, Lauralee Thompson, and Bill Klein spent many a happy hour counting these creatures near the Titusville bridge. There were others involved as well, particularly at one of the other sites on Merritt Island and a group of us gathered at our house to talk science and the lagoon. Lauralee also joined us for an event at our house hosting the A Rocha International team, Williams Baptist University team, and local supporters where she shared her knowledge of the local area having grown up in Titusville. That same year we began to volunteer with the Brevard Zoo's Restore Our Shores team and this has become a significant part of how we serve locally. We have also helped with the University of Central Florida's restoration work mostly helping with the mangrove nursery at the university, but also in the past planting mangroves for shoreline stabilization. The work of restoration in the lagoon needs huge numbers of people and organizations and I have been thankful to get to know a number of them and participate in oyster, clam, mangrove, and seagrass restoration efforts.

Restoration is an interesting word and though I mostly happily use it in many contexts, it does not sit well with me. There are two problems, at least: scientifically and theologically. Restoration implies making a judgment about what a place should be like by comparing the current state to some state in the past. The question is what state in the past? Do we use the experiences of someone local like Lauralee to help us understand what she experienced as a young person in the Indian River Lagoon? Do we go back to journals of European and American explorers and try to recreate those abundances and habitats? What about pre-colonization or even pre-initial colonization by American Indians as they too migrated to North America through a land bridge from Asia. I think we end up settling on a functional ecosystem with some semblance of health using biodiversity criterion – but we do have to choose and one species decides what that end point might be.

The theological issue relates to looking backward in time. The arrow of time goes forward in Christian terms towards the new creation, not backward towards a restoration of Eden. Some of the principles outlined in the Biblical creation myths (in the technical sense) give us some ideals, but the actual working out of these is interfaced with the city garden imagery of the final book of the Bible, Revelation. It becomes even less clear how exactly the early chapters of Genesis point us in a helpful direction when we integrate those texts with the scientific narrative. Some Christian ecologists have suggested Reconciliation Ecology as a helpful term indicating the central place of the cross in the healing of creation and our role as reconcilers. This seems to be more forward-looking, but the term has not really taken off and in reality, we can think of restoration as being future orientated. In a way what this does is let science and human choice decide on the actual details of the new creation in light of Biblical principles which emphasize the healing of all relationships that were broken.

What this looks like in the Indian River Lagoon is an interesting question. Here is something I wrote a few years ago to answer this question.

I sat talking with a friend who spends a lot of time on the water near my new home in Titusville, Florida. The Indian River Lagoon is one of the most biodiverse estuaries in the USA. However, under the water, the lagoon is dying. Recurrent algal blooms are causing the water to turn a muddy brown and green. This blocks light to seagrass and causes the manatees to move on to other feeding grounds. There is an expectation that soon there will be a major fish die-off in the lagoon as there has been in the past. So my friend's question to me as I was explaining to him about the work of A Rocha was, "What does it look like?" And the implied, "How do we get it done?"

"Kids must be taught about the world as it is, not as we would like it to be." So says Gene Simmons, lead singer of KISS in his book, ON POWER. I couldn't resist this little book as I perused the new book shelf at our local library. I wondered what he had to say about the subjects of money and power, particularly in light of his successes. And yes, I am still a KISS fan today, as they were my favorite band as a child. That probably explains a lot!

Is the answer to how to achieve change to seize power, usually through making lots of money, so that we can make changes? Accept things as they are for now, but scratch and claw our way to the top to be able to have enough power and money to be able to make those changes? I don't think so.

My favorite character in the Harry Potter series is Professor Dumbledore. In the sixth book, he takes Harry to try and convince a former Hogwarts professor to take up his old post. They arrive at the location where Horace Slughorn is staying and find it mostly in shambles. Chandeliers were destroyed, pictures broken, and furniture overturned. Dumbledore exposes Slughorn's ruse, and they begin to put the house back to right. A wand is waved and everything flies back into place, just like it was before. In the movie, it is even more obvious as Dumbledore finishes with a kindly smile and says, "That was fun."

We all wish the answer to problems in our lives, and in the lagoon, would be for God to wave the metaphysical equivalent of a magic wand and make everything right. Or, we imagine what we could do "if only"–if only systems would change, or if only we had more power. But Scripture teaches that this is not God's plan for the current time, for us, and where we are right now.

We see His answer in the death and resurrection of Jesus. God chose to work through sacrifice, suffering, and death – and yes, through new life. New creation is ushered in through our filling up what is lacking in Christ's afflictions (Colossians 1:24) in the here and now. It means saying no to plastic when it would be easier not to. It might mean not eating certain (or any) seafood. It means choosing to live in a sacrificial way, not only for other people but for our fellow creatures.

It also means living joyfully and in resurrection hope. Christ died so that we could have a relationship with God, but, at the cross, he also fixed all things that were broken in the fall. Scripture teaches that not only was our relationship with God broken, but also our relationships with each other, with creation, and even with ourselves. Christ's resurrection gives us hope for both people and the planet.

Resurrection hope for the Indian River Lagoon looks like clean water with healthy seagrass beds where manatees and sea turtles eat of the abundance. It looks like people experiencing the joy and wonder of a dolphin surfacing nearby, families enjoying each other and God through a beautiful place, fishermen catching enough to supply their needs, jobs created, and communities thriving around the lagoon. It looks like people experiencing God through a whole and healthy ecosystem. I am looking forward to being a part of that!

Most of my training and research have been in the tropics. Titusville sits at the border of the temperate and subtropical zones. This means that there is high biodiversity as the area is the southern end of the range for many species and habitats and the northern end of the range for other species. One of the habitats that is found locally – or rather is no longer found locally – is oyster reefs. The area used to support a major fishery for oysters which no longer exists due to taking too many. Oysters are mollusks, so related to clams and other bivalves meaning those mollusks have two shells which close together to protect the animal. Oysters like many marine organisms have external fertilization, so the eggs and sperm are shed into the water and the animals rely on mixing of large numbers doing this up in the water column for successful reproduction. The little oysters float up in the water column and are dragged around by currents and water circulation until they grow to a size where they are ready for a settled life. They then sense, amazingly for a tiny creature less than 1 mm long, a suitable place preferring oyster beds to join others. Overfishing not only reduces the total number of animals that can reproduce, it also reduces the ability of little ones to survive. When you take an oyster for food, you take the shell with you and open it later to eat.

One of the great joys of my time in Titusville has been volunteering with the Brevard Zoo Restore Our Shores team on their oyster reef restoration projects and more recently clam and seagrass restoration. I have to tell you, it is a lot easier to keep oyster reefs healthy and sustainable than to recreate them! The ROS team is doing a great job, but it is a major process. The shells must be collected from restaurants that have imported the animals to serve their customers from other places in the country. These shells must be seasoned and any remaining flesh rotted away so there are large fields that the team uses for this purpose with huge mounds of oyster shells. I have seen the changes in the design of the reefs over time as we have learned more about what works, but initially, we would in a large group take shovels and scoop up a bucket of shells and then bring it to a machine which would bring the shells by conveyer belt to a height where they could be dropped into a PVC tube with a mesh bag around the end. The person running the machine would allow enough shells in to fill the bag, remove the tube, which was only a conduit into the bag, and then pass off the mesh bag to another for securely tying. Some bags were left with fewer shells as these would be seeded with live oysters. At the end of the day, there were pallets and pallets of oyster shell bags that would be ready for use. But we also needed live oysters so that we could increase reproduction and you want to make sure that they are genetically compatible for the Indian River Lagoon. University labs were able to provide enough of what is called genetic broodstock to be able to supply these live oysters – but at a very small size. Another cadre of volunteers is oyster farmers. Those with access to water, a property on a canal, for example, could help by hanging bags of oysters off their dock until the animals get to the correct size. These are then collected at the right time and joined at a reef-building site by the shell bags made previously. Each bag that will have live oysters is opened, the live oysters added, and then re-tied. In the water, usually offshore of a private property where the owner has given permission to build the reef and all the permits needed from the appropriate authorities have been secured, then are laid on the bottom of the lagoon by more volunteers and staff. Initially, two rows of bags were laid on the bottom sans live oysters and then another on top with the live oysters. However, these need to be secured so that the next storm doesn't just tear it all up, so tie wraps need to be applied in between all the bags so that they keep together. You can see, conservation of these reefs would be a lot better than restoration! Alas, we lost our chance for conservation. The ROS team now uses metal gabions (metal cages) rather than plastic bags and continues to experiment with various designs to increase the probability of success.

It is interesting work and I try to have long-term interns take part in all aspects of the work. Our favorite part is probably the monitoring – because then you must go back and see how it is all working. We take a few bags off the reef, open them up, count live oysters, newly settled oysters, and all the creatures that are found using the reefs. Like coral reefs, oyster reefs provide a substrate and are an ecosystem engineer, creating space for other creatures to live. So, you have animals like sponges and bryozoans which colonize the surface of the oysters, and creatures like crabs, marine worms, and fish which live in and around the oyster reef seeking protection and food. The ROS team are fantastic people and hugely dedicated to the task. It has been a great joy to know them and many of the long-term volunteers who are amazing people as well. Collaboration and camaraderie in science is probably one of the least understood aspects of this type of career.

Much of my experience of the ocean and study of it has focused on animals at the higher end of the food chain. Something I didn't expect to learn about here in Titusville is the dramatic impact of nutrients impacting a system, in this case, the Indian River Lagoon. The population surrounding the lagoon has continued to rise with new building constantly. This not only exchanges vegetation for concrete but also brings people from other places who do not understand the impacts of their actions. Many come from the northern part of the USA where they had beautiful green lawns and this is still the standard of suburban perfection. However, to do that in Florida, you need not only species that didn't flourish here previously, but often loads of fertilizers, pesticides, and water. Additionally, much of the early building along the lagoon relied on septic tanks to deal with human waste. While this does a good job of removing much that is harmful, though not any pharmaceuticals that pass through your system, it does not remove basic nutrients like nitrogen and phosphorus. Additionally, any agriculture in the area is often heavily reliant on fertilizers and pesticides and even auto and truck exhaust puts out chemicals that end up in the lagoon.

Systems can often absorb these types of impacts for many years without noticeable changes. Then in one relatively short period of time, these systems can shift phases from one type of place to another. This can often be precipitated by natural events. A famous example is from the Caribbean where years and years of overfishing resulted in low fish grazing rates of algae on coral reefs. But sea urchins were able to fulfill the same function and though people noticed a lot more urchins on the reefs, the coral reef cover remained very similar, and these were coral-dominated systems. However, a natural pathogen went through the whole Caribbean, those damn currents again, and killed all the main grazing urchins. Very quickly the algae overgrew the coral and, in the places, where overfishing was worst, they shifted to algae-dominated systems. From the recorded history of the Indian River Lagoon, it had clear water with a bottom covered in seagrass that supported a huge fish community and the beloved manatee. Channels were built to drain Orlando for housing and brought nutrients and muck/sediment into the lagoon for many years along with the above-mentioned growth and changes in land use. The lagoon could keep up for a long time and then what appears to have happened is that an especially cold winter broke the system. This resulted in what is now called HABs – Harmful Algal Blooms – and the system began to change towards low water clarity, drift algae dominating, seagrass beds dying off, and populations of animals plummeting, including a record number of 1000+ manatees starving to death. Unfortunately, we can't just go back a little bit to return it to what it was, but often you have to significantly change the factors that are impacting things so that the negative effects are able to be dealt with again. We also don't understand the early impacts of overfishing species like oysters and clams and likely the top-level predators.

We remain hopeful in all things. Science tells us what the problems are and there are relatively simple solutions – the difficulty being that it means we need to change some of the ways we live and that is difficult. Humans are the problem, but they are also part of the solution. It has been and hopefully will continue to be a great privilege to be a small part of moving the Indian River Lagoon more towards what it will be in the New Creation – a place of flourishing for all species.

Author Bio

Dr Robert Sluka is a curious explorer, applying hopeful, optimistic and holistic solutions to all that is ailing our oceans and the communities that rely on them. Dabbling in theology, he writes on the interface between Christian faith and marine conservation. He has worked cross-culturally, living for extended periods in Australia, India, Great Britain, and his native USA. Robert's research focuses on marine biodiversity conservation, plastic pollution, and fisheries, particularly marine protected areas. The ultimate goal is to glorify God through oceans and communities being transformed through holistic marine conservation.

Robert's Ph.D. is from the University of Miami where he studied coral reef fish ecology. He subsequently spent ten years in South Asia researching the live fish food trade in Maldives and describing for the first time the rocky and coral reefs of the western coast of India. He then moved to the UK and focused on coastal ecology and began to work with A Rocha to develop their marine conservation program. This began with conservation on the Kenyan coast studying and protecting one of East Africa's oldest marine protected areas. Work on plastic pollution began on the south coast of France and in Portugal and now A Rocha globally combats plastic pollution through research and conservation efforts. Now based in Titusville Florida, in addition to continued work abroad, he leads conservation efforts to protect the northern Indian River Lagoon and coastal beaches.

More than 70 scientific publications on a variety of topics have informed science-based management and conservation of marine species globally. Robert's publications in theology have explored Christian themes as related to marine protected areas, plastic pollution, poverty, fisheries, and conservation generally. Locally in Florida, he studies the sandy beach ecology and impacts of plastic pollution along the Space Coast, Indian River Lagoon Biodiversity, and volunteers regularly with oyster reef, mangrove, and seagrass restoration efforts.

X @bobsluka

Instagram @bobsluka

Youtube @robertsluka1806

www.linkedin.com/in/robertdsluka

https://www.researchgate.net/profile/Robert-Sluka-3

https://sluka.substack.com

Made in the USA
Columbia, SC
24 October 2024

44499527R00074